PENGUIN BOOKS

20 MINUTES TO TOTAL FITNESS

Dr Shelly Batra was educated in La Martiniere Girls' School, Lucknow, and King George's Medical College, Lucknow. She specialized in Obstetrics and Gynaecology, and worked at the prestigious All India Institute of Medical Sciences, New Delhi. She is an Honorary Consultant for several hospitals in New Delhi, and her private practice focuses on high-risk pregnancy, women's health and fitness. She writes columns on health in newspapers and magazines, and is the author of *The Intimate Self: A Guide to Women's Sexual Health*. She has also appeared in several TV talk shows on health-related matters.

BY THE SAME AUTHOR

The Intimate Self: A Guide to Women's Sexual Health

20 Minutes to Total Fitness

DR SHELLY BATRA

PENGUIN BOOKS

Penguin Books India (P) Ltd., 11 Community Centre, Panchsheel Park, New Delhi 110 017, India
Penguin Books Ltd., 80 Strand, London, WC2R 0RL, UK
Penguin Putnam Inc., 375 Hudson Street, New York, NY 10014, USA
Penguin Books Australia Ltd., 250 Camberwell Road, Camberwell, Victoria 3124, Australia
Penguin Books Canada Ltd., 10 Alcorn Avenue, Suite 300, Toronto, Ontario, M4V 3B2, Canada
Penguin Books (NZ) Ltd., Cnr Rosedale & Airborne Roads, Albany, Auckland, New Zealand

First published by Penguin Books India 2002

10 9 8 7 6 5 4 3 2 1

Typeset in Dante MT by Eleven Arts, New Delhi
Printed at Chaman Offset Printers, New Delhi

Inside illustrations by Prithvishwar Gayan.

Dedicated to my father, who showed
that physical fitness and professional excellence
go hand in hand.

Contents

Introduction

'*Mens sana in corpore sano*' (a fit mind in a fit body) sums up our concept of fitness. Fitness, in general understanding, is synonymous with strength and stamina, and the ability to fight both disease and depression. Technically, fitness involves measures and levels of muscular ability and endurance, heart action and its response to activity, agility, balance, coordination, etc. But fitness is not just about objective figures—it is also a personal thing. A fit person is not just physically healthy, he or she is also mentally well-adjusted, emotionally balanced, and well-adapted to his or her own social milieu.

Fitness is thus one's ability to work with vigour and pleasure, without undue fatigue, with energy left over at the end of the day for enjoying hobbies and recreation, and of course, a feeling of all-pervasive well-being throughout the day.

Research has shown that a physically fit person is able to withstand fatigue for longer periods of time than the unfit, and is better equipped to tolerate physical stress. Physical fitness is directly related to mental alertness and absence of nervous tension. Weak muscles are a major cause of sagging abdomens and flabby looks; weak bones and muscles together cause almost ninety per cent of the cases of chronic backache. One of the most important reasons for being fit is that only then is it possible to have the fullest enjoyment of living.

Prehistoric man had to hunt for food. He had to walk for miles, climb trees and carry loads. There were few mechanical aids to make his work easier. However, as civilization advances, lifestyles become sedentary. Our grandparents probably ground wheat, drew water from wells, helped in the fields, and walked much longer distances to go to places. Today, however, automation, increasing mechanization and work-saving devices that make life easy deprive us of desirable physical activity. It is necessary for us to return to the more active lifestyles of forefathers if we want to avoid disease and disability. Exercise over and above the normal demands of daily living is today essential for the development of an efficient, durable and strong body, and it is with this aim in mind that this book has been written.

In this day and age, there can be no excuse for being obese or unfit. Our consciousness of the need to be fit is constantly reinforced through the media. There is emphasis on adopting lifelong habits which are conducive to health and fitness. Weight loss, while desirable, should not be the main goal. As awareness of the need for being fit spreads, so has the facilities that enable us to do so.

Too often, despite our best intentions, getting fit and staying fit remain elusive goals. Most of us would like to be fitter than we are at present. But we are uncertain of what is the best method for us, and find it difficult to think of adding one more thing to our busy schedules. What is required is determination, effort and strong will power. In the quest for fitness, as with many other things, it is easy to slip up.

If you are physically fit, you feel better, look better and work better. Strength and endurance improve with regular and modulated exercise. This book shows you how—for as little as 20 minutes a day—you are conscientious and regular, you too can become fit and gain strength, endurance and flexibility. Each of us should train ourselves so that our bodies can attain the highest level of efficiency, and each of us can realize our fullest potential. This book, encompassing every aspect of exercise and fitness, shows you how to achieve this goal

New Delhi
May 2002

Dr Naresh Trehan
Executive Director and Chief
Cardio Thoracic Surgeon,
Escorts Heart Institute and
Medical Research Centre

The Basics

The Importance of Exercise

Exercise is any rhythmical activity which elevates the heart rate above resting levels, and involves the use of a single large muscle group, or the coordinated use of several muscle groups. It includes walking, cycling, skating, jogging, aerobic dancing, climbing stairs, rowing, skating, weight lifting and participation in sports and athletic activities.

Exercise has manifold benefits: most importantly, it increases the total daily energy expenditure. One uses calories or energy in order to exercise, and if this increase in energy expenditure is not directly offset by a corresponding increase in energy intake, weight loss or weight maintenance will be achieved.

Exercise results in toning up of all the body systems. If you live in a city and work in an office or at home, chances are that your daily schedule includes minimal physical activity, food is abundant and readily available, and you consume a fair share of high calorie, refined foods, loaded with sugar and fats. You probably regard exercise as something of a chore, which you know you should do regularly but for various reasons seldom do.

Yet if you dedicate a mere 20 minutes of each day, about three to five times a week, the benefits you derive are enormous. Twenty minutes is nothing: it is the time you spend stuck in rush-hour traffic, or watching a TV serial which you don't really want to see but which you end up watching because it is sandwiched between two of your favourites. In the whole week you would devote less time to exercise than you would to watching a film. Yet the benefits you reap can change your whole life.

What are the benefits of exercise?

1. Improves your figure

Today a lot of emphasis—some of it unnecessary—is laid on looking good. Many people exercise for figure enhancement, or to maintain their bodies in their current shape. Most of us feel we could lose an inch here or an inch there, tummies could be flatter or thighs trimmer. Exercise burns fat deposits all over the body. More importantly, it tones up the muscles, so the bulges of fat become less prominent.

When you begin exercising, it will not immediately result in weight loss. This is because as you start working out, the fat in your body decreases in amount and muscle mass increases. Fat is *not* converted to muscle actually but muscle mass increases, so it seems as if fat is being converted to muscles. In reality, fat is being *replaced* by muscle. If you weigh yourself approximately two weeks after starting an exercise programme, your weight will be the same as before, and may actually be a little higher. Muscle is more dense than fat, so for the same volume, muscle weighs more than fat. But the benefits to your shape will soon be visible. If you measure your waist, hips and thighs, there will be a slight decrease in the measurements.

Inch loss comes before fat loss, and improved muscle tone is responsible for this phenomenon. If you are exercising you will have trimmer thighs than someone who is not, even though the fat content may be the same. You start looking trimmer, even though you may weigh the same as before.

2. Best treatment for obesity and related disorders

Exercise is a much better treatment than dieting for obesity and related problems. If you are overweight, a starvation diet may not be the solution. Faced with such a diet, the body automatically slows down the metabolic rate. When you are on a starvation diet, your body is like a fire sustained with very little fuel.

Your chances of weight loss are much greater if you eat a moderate diet and exercise. Exercise speeds up the body's metabolism, so the food eaten is consumed faster, and fat deposition does not take place.

Exercise helps in controlling many of the medical problems connected with obesity. With exercise, the ill effects of these diseases are stayed, if not actually reversed. Doctors find it is easy to control medical problems with minimal medication. For example:

- Exercise controls the blood pressure.
- In diabetics, it increases insulin sensitivity—less insulin has a greater effectiveness in lowering blood sugar levels. Exercise burns up the blood sugars, so diabetes is automatically improved.
- Regular physical activity has a favourable effect on high cholesterol levels.

A word of caution

Many medical disorders are far more common in obese individuals, such as high blood pressure, increased incidence of coronary disease, diabetes mellitus, strokes, osteoarthritis, sleep apnoea (a condition where sleep is interrupted by short spells of breathlessness), gall stones, and cancers of the colon, breast, gall bladder and uterus.

Studies on the relationship of obesity and physical activity indicate that obese schoolchildren eat less, weigh more, and are less active than other children. They spend less time in physical activity, and if at all they do so, they prefer to engage in less strenuous activities. They lack stamina, they tire easily, and because of their sheer bulk, they require more energy to do the same activity as compared to lean children.

Obesity and lack of physical activity are interrelated. Reduced activity leads to obesity. And obesity itself results in decreased work tolerance, so that obese persons lack the ability and the desire to be physically active. In other words, once a person gains excess weight, a vicious cycle is set in, whereby physical activity decreases as a direct consequence of obesity, leading to further weight gain. The only way to break this vicious cycle is by exercise. Frequent and regular exercise will cause an increase in energy expenditure that exceeds energy intake, and the end result will be weight loss.

The ideal exercises for an obese person are, at least initially, low-intensity ones like walking. However, high-intensity exercises have more benefits. They promote not only substantial weight and fat loss but also increase certain enzymes in the muscles which promote oxidation of energy, which continues even during non-exercising periods, leading to further loss.

A word of caution

Exercises in general are more difficult for obese people because they experience difficulty in doing them and also because their metabolism limits prolonged physical work. High-intensity exercises may not be tolerated well by severely obese persons, at least initially, because they will be unable to exercise for long periods of time. High-impact exercises put a strain on the joints, which adds to the difficulty. Vigorous exercise is unsafe for those who have cardiovascular problems or backache.

3. Toning of the neuromuscular system

Exercise strengthens muscles so that your capacity to work increases tremendously. Regular and sustained exercise, be it high intensity or low intensity, results in building up stamina. The body gains strength and flexibility, and is less prone to injury. Vague aches and pains, which seem to be altogether too common in all age groups, tend to disappear with regular exercise.

A 30-year-old housewife started swimming regularly. After a month, she says, 'Earlier I would feel tired carrying a 2-kilogram shopping bag. Now I can carry 10 kilograms of freshly ground flour from the mill without feeling it!'

Exercise improves muscles in seven ways:

- The strength of a muscle, which is the amount of force the muscle can exert, increases. This depends on the size and number of muscle fibres that can be brought into action at one time. Increasing strength enhances your capacity for physical exertion.
- The endurance of a muscle, which is its ability to repeat an action over and over again, or to sustain a muscular contraction, is enhanced. Endurance is also dependent upon the functioning of the cardiovascular systems, and its ability to transport food and oxygen to the muscles.
- The speed response of a muscle is improved, which leads to better reflexes. This is due to metabolic and neuromuscular toning up of the skeletal system.
- The total mass of a muscle is increased.
- Blood supply to muscle fibres is increased as exercise tones up the circulatory system, with the heart pumping blood faster, and propelling greater amount of blood per beat. A large quantity of circularity blood is diverted to the muscles involved in exercise.
- There is enhanced oxidative capacity, which means that the body's ability to utilize glucose and related substances in order to release energy, is increased.
- There is a shift towards a greater percentage of Type I fibres (see below). This is a long-term adaptation to regular exercise.

There are two types of muscle fibre, which have different contractile and metabolic properties:

Type I or slow-twitch fibres: **These have a high oxidative rate, i.e., they rapidly utilize and burn up energy.**

Type II or fast-twitch fibres: **These have a low oxidative potential. They are slow in burning calories. People who are sedentary have a high proportion of these.**

All this leads to efficient, rapid and enhanced energy consumption by the muscles during and after exercise.

Muscle fitness is a direct consequence of exercise. Both the structure and the function of skeletal muscles improve with exercise; both metabolic and morphological fitness can be achieved.

4. Improvement in cardio-respiratory functions

A healthy heart pumps more blood per stroke than an unhealthy one, so that in order to circulate the same amount of blood through the body, the number of beats required is less. This reflects in a lowering of the pulse or heart rate. Athletes have been found to have pulse rates as low as fifty-six beats per minute, while those who lead a sedentary lifestyle have rapid pulses, even up to eighty-five beats per minute.

Increase in aerobic power is achieved through exercise only. Intense exercise can place an enormous metabolic demand on the body, which needs more oxygen, more glucose, and an increased supply of metabolic substrates (substances in the body that are oxidized to release energy, such as glucose, glycogen, body fat in those who exercise regularly, and in starvation patients even muscle protein). The heart, lungs, circulatory and respiratory systems are involved in the process of supplying oxygen to the tissues, and the removal of carbon dioxide and metabolic by-products from the body. These body systems gain strength and efficiency as a result of exercise.

A number of studies have proved conclusively that regular physical exercise is beneficial for the heart in the following ways:

- Endurance exercise training, or exercise which involves running, swimming or cycling can lead to a remarkable increase in the prowess of the cardiovascular system. The cardiac output increases, the pulse rate decreases, and the body's ability to consume oxygen increases greatly.

Stroke volume =	amount of blood pumped per beat.
Cardiac output=	stroke volume x heart rate
=	volume of blood pumped by the heart per minute (given in ml/minute)

- Endurance training improves blood lipid profile. The total circulating lipids, cholesterol and triglycerides decrease with exercise, leading to less clogging of the blood vessels with fat deposits.

Lipids (fats) in blood

Triglycerides

LDL = Low density lipoproteins VLDL = Very low density lipoproteins		These are harmful as they get deposited in the blood vessels leading to hardening and narrowing of arteries.

Cholesterol

HDL = High density lipoproteins	These are beneficial as they cause cholesterol to be transferred to the liver, where it can be metabolized. They help in clearing the blood vessels and tissues of fat deposits.

- Atherosclerosis, or hardening of the arteries, which is directly responsible for high blood pressure and heart attacks, comes to a standstill, and may even reverse in some individuals.
- The HDL or high density lipoproteins which protect the heart from coronary artery disease increase with exercise. So the beneficial lipids in the blood increase, and the harmful lipids decrease.
- Exercise increases the size and number of blood vessels, leading to better circulation, and increased oxygen supply to cells.
- Exercise increases the elasticity of blood vessels, which then give less resistance to the blood flow. This results in the blood pressure falling when patients are put on regular exercise.

All these factors combined minimize your chances of getting a heart attack. Sedentary people have a 30–40 per cent higher risk of dying from coronary problems than those who exercise moderately.

When you exercise, your respiratory system undergoes structural as well as functional adaptations. While exercising, the lungs are forced to expand to their fullest during inhalation. During expiration all the vestiges of stale air are compressed and squeezed out. Thus lung functions improve and lung capacity is enhanced. This is why patients of tuberculosis, bronchial asthma and obstructive lung disease are put on carefully monitored exercise programmes.

While exercising, both the heart rate and the respiratory rate go up in order to meet the added oxygen requirement of the muscles, and thus circulation also improves.

5. Improves the muscular-skeletal system

- Exercise increases the protein and mineral content of bones and makes them firm and strong.
- Exercise aids in the proper growth of bones and muscles in children, and allows a child to attain maximum height.
- Exercise improves the posture. Those who exercise tend not to slouch, and they gain almost half an inch in height just by standing erect.
- Exercise improves endurance and muscle coordination, and makes a person appear poised, graceful, and elegant.
- Disuse of muscles leads to atrophy. A bedridden patient loses muscle mass and strength, and lack of exercise results in calcium melting away from bones, leading to osteoporosis or weak and porous bones.
- After the age of 30, there is a natural tendency to weakness of the bones. Exercise actually promotes deposition of calcium in the bones.
- Middle-aged and elderly people and post-menopausal women have a tendency to develop bone pains or osteoporosis, and there is a grave risk of developing fractures with trivial trauma due to weak and fragile bones. All these risks can be counteracted by regular exercise.

6. Results in release of endorphins

Endorphins, or endogenous morphins, are morphine-like substances, but more powerful, released from the pituitary gland. This is called the master gland as it produces a large number of hormones which regulate body functions and the functioning of other endocrine glands in the body. Endorphins result in a feeling of well-being and sometimes even euphoria. They also have a pain-relieving effect, which explains why some individuals can go through gruelling intensive training, especially those who go for competitive sports.

There are stories legion about athletes who continued to run marathons even after having sprained their ankles or pulled a ligament. Will power of course is a large part of such effort, but the endorphins released due to exercise also help to dull the pain.

Indirectly, endorphins are partly responsible for exercise addiction. People whose bodies are used to exercise may develop a craving for it, not unlike that for alcohol or tobacco.

7. Results in healing

Exercise has tremendous healing powers. Physiotherapy is now a highly developed science, and a part of the recovery process for many diverse illnesses. Physiotherapists work closely with physicians and surgeons to prevent complications and promote healing through exercise.

Most post-operative patients tend to get backache or some degree of muscle stiffness due to enforced bed rest, which can be avoided by graded exercises. There are many orthopedic conditions, where progressively increasing exercises are a must. Even patients with slipped disc are expected to follow an exercise plan, even though they may be on bed rest for a prescribed period of time. This is because exercise promotes healing of certain tissues, strengthens others, and prevents disuse atrophy of whole groups of muscles.

8. The best sedative

Insomnia? Forget about warm milk and bedtime reading. Research has shown that even moderate exercise is followed by an all-pervading feeling of pleasurable well-being, which ultimately leads to restful sleep. Several studies have compared the effect of exercise with that of placebos in inducing and sustaining sleep, and exercise has proved to be beneficial.

Any form of exercise relieves tension, both physical and mental, and thus acts as a natural tranquillizer, which has the added advantage of having no side effects. Also, contrary to popular belief, exercise actually gets rid of body fatigue.

Many insomniacs find it easy to drop off to sleep if they take a brisk walk before bedtime, or do some similar physical activity.

9. Combats depression

Patients in psychiatric wards are encouraged by therapists to take up some form of exercise, such as walking, dancing or yoga. Psychiatrists have found that patients who exercise regularly require less medication than those who do not, and what is more important, the severity of their symptoms seems to decrease. This is especially true of patients who suffer from depression, both endogenous (depression with no known precipitating factor) and reactive (depression in response to external factors).

10. Slows down the ageing process

Moderate, regular and sustained exercise has the effect of slowing down or even arresting the ageing process. Large, obese and sluggish individuals tend to look older than their years, while those who are physically fit tend to look younger.

All the organ systems of the body, including the nervous system, are influenced by exercise, and mental capacity, memory and intelligence all benefit.

11. General overall sense of well-being

Exercise gives self-confidence and improves self-discipline. Those who exercise develop a high degree of physical stamina, with increased mental alertness. Exercise develops organizing ability, resilience, the will power to cope with setbacks and injuries, and high levels of perseverance and dedication, which are of immense value in all walks of life.

Another long-term effect of exercise is to suppress the appetite. Those who have a tendency to overeat or indulge in snacking find that after working out regularly for a while, they are less inclined to do so.

12. Tones the body

When you are do not exercise regularly, then in a state of relaxation you have a very small pool of circulating fuels, say about 100 kcal, that are available to meet your demands. If used in its entirety, this is sufficient to allow you to play 15 minutes of tennis or do 20 minutes of brisk walking.

Blood glucose is the main substance in circulation that is consumed by the body tissues to provide energy. That amount of glucose that can provide 100 kcal of energy is circulatory in the blood in the resting stage. This is a miniscule amount as compared to the huge amounts of energy required during vigorous exercise.

Metabolic changes during exercise require the mobilization of huge quantities of metabolic substrates. Glycogen stores in the muscles and liver are used up rapidly, and then the enormous store of adipose tissue or body fat is mobilized. The entire machinery of the human body swings into action, secretions by the neural and endocrine systems get activated, the liver, muscles and fat tissue get energized, the heart pumps rapidly and the respiratory rate goes up, blood circulates at a tremendous speed, and the face appears flushed and skin becomes warm. Physiological and hormonal adaptations to exercise tone up every system of the body, with an overall beneficial effect.

Some the more common reasons why people do not exercise are often ones which can be got around with a little bit of creative thinking:

Where do you find the time?

Many people find it difficult to fit in time for exercise into their busy schedules. They are far too busy with their jobs, or they have demanding babies or sick parents or children to take care of. But you can always try one of the following:

- Get up half an hour early. Not only do you breathe in unadulterated fresh air, free from pollutants, you also start the day with a positive attitude and a feeling of well-being.
- Use your lunch break to exercise. Have a light lunch of fruit and a sandwich or a chappati about 2 hours before the normal lunch break.
- If you have more free time in the evening, exercise after you come home from work. Many people are more relaxed after they are done with the day's work. If you go out in the evening often, you can work out at the gym or pool, shower and change there and go for your evening's entertainment directly. Exercise relaxes and refreshes you, and you will enjoy the evening more.
- Be realistic. Set realistic goals. A little exercise is better than none. If you cannot fit in 20 minutes at one stretch anywhere in your schedule, break it up into two 10-minute capsules, or three 7-minute ones. This will give you the same fat loss benefits, though the cardiovascular benefit will not be as much as it is with a sustained 20-minute workout.
- Have business meetings or meet up with friends at the swimming pool or on the jogging track.
- Exercise at your workplace. You can do isometric exercises at your desk, or while sitting in front of a computer. Take a short break—and a short walk—every hour. Walk to the water cooler or the coffee machine instead of asking for it to be delivered to your desk. Run your errands within the office yourself.
- If you have a busy working week, exercise on weekends and fit in 20 minutes one day during the week. While ideally you should do five sessions of exercise per week, even three is better than none.
- Make exercise a family affair. Parents, children and grandchildren can all exercise together. An evening out could very well be a trip to the nearest sports centre. Most sports clubs have a wide spectrum of facilities, so that each person can find something

that suits his or her temperament. You get to spend quality time with your family, and improve your health at the same time.

- Combine exercise with a pleasurable activity. You can exercise in front of the TV, while your favourite programme is going on.
- Walk as much as you can. Do not take the car out for short trips. Do not use the remote control. Get up and take what you want. Do not be dependent on maids and servants to answer the doorbell or the phone. Take your dog out for a walk. Push your baby's pram—this will give you a good cardiovascular workout. Park your car half a mile away from your destination and walk.
- Make exercise a way of life. Take the stairs instead of waiting for the lift.
- Keep moving. People who are fidgety by nature tend to be more fit than their more sluggish counterparts.

Where do you find the energy?

When you are tired after housework and office work, you may feel that though you have the desire to exercise, you lack the energy reserves to do so. If you do manage to summon up the energy one day, the following few days your exhaustion levels are even higher, so that you cannot continue exercising.

Some people might also suffer from lack of energy due to poor nutrition. But often the cause is simply that when you begin working out, your body is not accustomed to exertion, the muscles lack tone, and your stamina is low.

- Check that your diet is adequate and balanced.
- Start slowly. If necessary, start with as little as 5 minutes a day. Gradually you will find that you are not so tired when you finish and will be able to exercise a bit longer.
- Initially, take breaks whenever you feel tired.
- Stop exercising if you experience more than an ache in your muscles.

As the days pass, the feeling of fatigue will pass and you will paradoxically feel more energetic after you finish exercising. You will be filled with a sense of strength and vitality.

Exercise builds up stamina. Researchers have found that those who exercise regularly perform better at work or at school as compared to those who don't.

Isn't it easier to lose weight by dieting?

Diet control can make you lose weight, but you miss out on the other benefits of exercise discussed above. If weight loss is your goal, then you should combine a moderate diet with plenty of exercise.

- Do not starve yourself. Starvation lowers the metabolism, so you actually burn calories at a slower rate. An obese person with a low metabolism can maintain his weight, even though his intake seems barely adequate. Exercise speeds up metabolism, so you burn calories faster.
- Diets work, but only as long as they last.
- A person who is overweight but exercises regularly is more fit than a person whose weight is normal, but who does not exercise at all.

Losing weight is like pushing a truck. It requires a lot of effort initially, but once you get going, it becomes progressively easy.

Assessing Your Fitness Level

Fit or unfit, this is the question that seems to worry most of us, yet what constitutes fit is hard to define precisely. It is about how you feel about your appearance, and how you feel when you get up in the morning; how tired you are after a hard day's work, and how eagerly—or half-heartedly—you look at things that need to be done. It is also about how you adjust to peers and siblings, and how you respond to the pressures and stresses of day to day living. Practically speaking, there is no one single parameter of fitness, for fitness is not just about weight or figure or muscle mass.

The word fitness encompasses physical, mental, emotional and even spiritual well being. You should know what the parameters that constitute fitness are, and be able to asses yourself.

Some of the parameters of judging fitness are:

How do you look?

Few of us are satisfied with our appearance. Most of us would like to weigh a little less, or bulge a little less in certain quarters, and we sigh over pictures of lithe and lissome models and sports persons. Surveys have shown that most fit persons, when asked how much weight they would like to lose, say 1 or 2 kilograms only, whereas most other people would not be happy with anything less than a 5-kilogram loss. Fit people are usually happy with their body image and weight.

The shape of your body is controlled by the bony frame of the skeleton, as well as the overlying muscles and fat. You cannot do anything about the frame which sets certain limits to how much you can change your body shape, but you can, and should, do something about the fat and the muscle.

Both fat and muscle are essential for the body. Fat is a vital ingredient of body tissue. It softens the contours of the body and gives it a rounded look. It helps to keep the body temperature constant; and acts as a storehouse of energy. Fat lines and protects the vital internal organs. When this storage fat becomes excessive in amount it gives an obese look, and because of its deposits in areas such as blood vessels, it becomes a health hazard.

Active persons utilize their muscles, so that they retain their pleasing firmness, called muscle tone. The less you exercise the softer and flabbier you become. With lack of exercise, muscle mass actually decreases, and muscles becomes small, flabby and less elastic. Flabbiness of muscles can ruin the appearance of individuals who are otherwise good looking.

The group of muscles which are the most problematic for a large majority are abdomen muscles. Taut abdominal muscles perform the same functions as a girdle, they hold the abdominal organs in place, and because of their tensile strength, they give the abdomen a flat appearance. In other parts of the body, taut muscles make fat less noticeable. A person who is exercising will have trimmer thighs than one who is not, even though the fat content may be the same. Improved muscle tone is responsible for this phenomenon.

With regular exercise, muscle mass increases, and one's weight may even increase a little. A slight weight gain may occur in the first few weeks of starting exercise. This can be due to increased muscle mass and increased appetite, but there is no need to get disheartened and stop exercise, for weight loss will certainly follow—howsoever gradually it may occur—in the days to come.

Appearance gives an indication, albeit a small one, about your level of fitness. Examine yourself in a full-length mirror.

- Do you look fat and pasty?
- Are there unseemly bulges?
- Do you have a spare tyre around your waist?
- Are you looking painfully thin and malnourished, with arms and legs like walking sticks?

Just by close observation you can decide for yourself whether you are fit or unfit. However, it is important to use more objective parameters.

How much do you weigh?

How much you should weigh depends on your height, build and gender.

The Indian Council for Medical Research has prepared charts, both for men and for women, which show what your weight should be. These

HEIGHT–WEIGHT CHART: Women

Height		*Weight*		
Metres	*Feet*	*Kgs (Small Frame)*	*Kgs (Medium Frame)*	*Kgs (Large Frame)*
1.49	4′11″	47.2–50.4	49.9–53.5	53.1–57.6
1.52	5′0″	47.6–51.3	50.8–54.4	54.0–58.5
1.55	5′1″	48.5–52.2	51.7–55.3	54.9–59.4
1.57	5′2″	49.9–53.5	53.1–56.7	56.2–61.2
1.60	5′3″	51.3–54.9	54.4–58.1	57.6–62.6
1.63	5′4″	52.6–56.7	56.2–59.9	59.4–64.4
1.65	5′5″	54.0–58.1	57.6–61.2	60.3–65.8
1.68	5′6″	55.8–59.9	59.0–63.5	62.6–68.0
1.70	5′7″	57.2–61.7	60.8–65.3	64.4–69.9
1.73	5′8″	58.5–63.1	62.2–66.7	65.8–71.7
1.75	5′9″	60.3–64.9	64.0–68.5	67.6–73.5
1.78	5′10″	61.7–66.7	68.8–70.3	69.0–75.3
1.80	5′11″	63.1–68.0	67.1–71.7	70.3–76.7

HEIGHT–WEIGHT CHART: Men				
Height		*Weight*		
Metres	*Feet*	*Kgs (Small Frame)*	*Kgs (Med. Frame)*	*Kgs (Large Frame)*
1.57	5'2"	52.6–56.7	56.2–60.3	59.4–64.4
1.60	5'3"	54.0–58.1	57.6–61.7	60.3–65.3
1.63	5'4"	55.3–59.9	59.0–63.5	62.2.67.6
1.65	5'5"	57.2.61.7	60.8–65.3	64.0–69.4
1.68	5'6"	58.5–63.1	62.2–66.7	65.8–71.2
1.70	5'7"	60.3–64.9	64.0–68.5	67.6–73.5
1.73	5'8"	61.7–66.7	65.8–70.7	69.4–75.3
1.75	5'9"	63.5–68.5	67.6–72.6	71.2–77.1
1.78	5'10"	65.3–70.3	69.4–74.4	73.0–79.4
1.80	5'11"	67.1–72.1	71.2–76.2	74.9–81.7
1.83	6'0"	69.0–74.4	73.0–78.5	76.7–83.9
1.85	6'1"	71.2–76.7	75.3–80.7	78.9–86.2
1.88	6'2"	73.9–79.4	77.6–83.5	81.2–88.9
190	6'3"	76.2–81.7	79.8–85.7	83.5–91.6

give a reasonable idea of whether you are overweight or underweight, and by how much.

But weight alone is by no means a complete assessment of fitness. You may have the ideal body weight, but your muscle tone or cardiac status may leave a lot to be desired.

What is your body mass index?

Body mass index (BMI) is a fairly good indicator of your nutritional status, and it correlates better with propensity to disease than weight alone. It is measured by dividing your weight (in kilograms) by the square of your height (in metres).

$$\text{BMI} = \frac{\text{Weight}}{\text{Height}^2}$$

A BMI of 19 to 24 is considered good, while a BMI of 25 to 29.5 indicates that the person is overweight, if not obese. A BMI of 29 or more is

Height	*Good BMI*						*Borderline BMI*				*Increasing Risk BMI*		
cm	*19*	*20*	*21*	*22*	*23*	*24*	*25*	*26*	*27*	*28*	*29*	*30*	*35*
	Weight in Kg												
140	37	39	41	43	45	47	49	51	53	55	57	59	69
142	38	40	42	44	46	48	50	52	54	57	60	61	71
144	39	42	44	46	48	50	52	54	56	58	60	62	73
146	41	43	45	47	49	51	53	55	58	60	62	64	75
148	42	44	46	48	50	53	55	57	60	61	64	66	77
150	43	45	47	50	52	54	56	59	61	63	65	68	79
152	44	46	49	51	53	55	58	60	62	65	67	69	81
154	45	47	50	52	55	57	59	62	64	67	69	71	83
156	46	49	51	54	56	58	61	63	66	68	71	73	85
158	47	50	52	55	57	60	62	65	67	70	72	75	87
160	49	51	54	56	59	61	64	67	69	72	74	77	90
162	50	53	55	58	60	63	66	68	71	74	76	79	92
164	51	54	57	59	62	65	67	70	73	75	78	81	94
166	52	55	58	61	63	66	69	72	74	77	80	83	96
168	54	56	59	62	65	68	71	73	76	79	82	85	99
170	55	58	61	64	67	69	72	75	78	81	84	87	101
172	56	59	62	65	68	71	74	77	80	83	86	89	104
174	58	61	64	67	70	73	76	79	82	85	88	91	106
176	59	62	65	68	71	74	77	81	84	87	90	93	108
178	60	63	67	70	73	76	79	82	86	89	92	95	111
180	62	65	68	71	75	78	81	84	88	91	94	97	113
182	63	66	69	73	76	80	83	86	89	93	96	99	116
184	64	68	71	75	78	81	85	88	91	95	98	102	119
186	66	69	73	76	80	83	87	90	93	97	100	104	121
188	67	70	74	78	81	85	88	92	95	99	103	106	124
190	69	72	76	79	83	87	98	94	97	101	105	108	126

proof of gross obesity, with a very high risk of cardiovascular and other disorders. Research has shown that the BMI correlates significantly with body fat, illness and mortality, and is a better prognostic indicator than body weight alone.

What is your percentage of body fat?

The percentage of body fat in healthy humans ranges from 5 to 40 per cent. Women have more body fat than men.

While dietary practices and nutritional supplementation are obviously important in controlling this, exercise, especially some form of resistance exercise, is also crucial.

While most people have too much fat (chronic obesity is the point at which your overweight condition is considered a disease), the reverse is also a problem. For women, body fat should not be less than 15 per cent and for men, not less than 5 percent. Excess dieting can cause loss of muscle mass and strength along with fat. Most athletes perform best in the low fat rather than the very low fat range.

Fat Level	*Men*	*Women*
Very low	Below 5%	below 15%
Low	5–13%	15–20%
Average	13–17%	20–25%
High	17–20%	25–27%
Clinical obesity	20–27%	28–31%
Chronic obesity	28% and above	32% and above

There are several ways of measuring body fat:

- Measuring skin-fold thickness with calipers.
- Hydrostatic weighing, where a person's underwater weight is compared with his dry-land weight to determine body density, which is inversely proportional to body fat.
- The impedance system, which measures the body's resistance to electrical current. This test is an accurate reflection of lean body mass and thus a good way to estimate total body fat.

Most health clubs have the facilities to measure body fat percentage.

What is your waist circumference?

Absolute measurements of the waistline have been found to correlate well with a tendency to cardiovascular disease and overall fitness. Waist circumference is essentially a method of measuring abdominal fat. People who are pot-bellied, or those who have a thick roll of fat hanging around the waist like a tyre are the ones most susceptible to ischemic heart disease or angina, even though they may have a total body weight which is within the accepted limits.

The following values of waist circumference are considered satisfactory:

For women	Less than 88 centimetres
For men	Less than 92 centimetres

To measure the waist circumference:

- Stand comfortably in front of a mirror, either undressed, or wearing a thin shirt without elastic bands pressing into the skin.
- Breathe normally. Do not suck in your breath and make an effort to pull in the abdomen.
- Place your hands by your sides, and try and locate the lower border of the rib cage.
- Move your hands down, and try and feel the upper border of the hip bone, also known as the iliac crest.
- Measure your waist circumference at a point midway between the lower border of the rib cage and the iliac crest.

What is your waist-hip ratio?

If there is a high waist-hip ratio, or in other words, the waist measures more than the hip, it indicates a degree of unfitness. High waist-hip ratios correlate directly with heart disease.

The American Heart Association has declared that a waist-hip ratio of more than 1.0 for men, and more than 0.85 for women is significant, and can be positively dangerous if left unattended.

What is your resting pulse rate?

Your heart rate is a direct measure of your cardiac status. The stronger the heart, the lower will be the rate at which it pumps blood.

The pulse offers the easiest identifiable measure of your heart rate and although taking the pulse will be tricky at first, with practice, it becomes easy. Except in certain cardiac disorders, the heart rate is equivalent to the pulse rate, so one of the best ways to assess the functioning of the heart would be to take the pulse rate.

Your pulse is a pulsating blood vessel that lies close to the surface in the body, and can be easily felt or palpated. The heart pumps blood several times a minute into a large blood vessel called the aorta, from where it goes into smaller blood vessels called arteries. Arteries carry oxygenated blood from the heart to all parts of the body, where oxygen is utilized, carbon dioxide is released, and the de-oxygenated blood is brought back to the heart through blood vessels called the veins. Each time the heart pumps blood, a gush of blood is felt in the arteries in the form of a pulse.

Your resting pulse rate (RPR) is an excellent indicator of the efficiency of your heart muscles and your fitness level as a whole. To take the RPR, take your pulse rate early in the morning, just after getting up from bed, when you are relaxed and before the stresses of the day have started taking a toll on you.

How do you take your pulse?

You will need a watch with a seconds hand.

To feel the pulse at the wrist (also called the radial pulse), place your left hand on the table with the palm facing upward. Now place the index, middle and ring fingers of the right hand on the

wrist, just beneath the thumb, in a vertical line. You can feel the throb of an artery beneath your fingers. Count the number of throbs per minute to get your RPR.

Similarly, you can feel a pulse at the front of the elbow (the brachial pulse) or just beneath the angle of the jaw (the carotid pulses).

Nowadays there are different kinds of pulse monitors in the market which help to take your pulse. You must follow the directions given with the apparatus.

As a general principle, the stronger the heart, the lower is the RPR. This is because a strong heart can pump huge quantities of blood in every thrust, so the number of times it needs to pump blood is less.

RPR: Men				
Age	*Poor*	*Fair*	*Good*	*Excellent*
20–29	86+	70–84	62–68	60 or less
30–39	86+	72–84	64–70	62 or less
40–49	90+	74–88	66–72	64 or less
50+	90+	76–88	68–74	66 or less

RPR: Women				
Age	*Poor*	*Fair*	*Good*	*Excellent*
20–29	96+	78–94	72–76	70 or less
30–39	98+	80–96	72–78	70 or less
40–49	100+	80–98	74–78	72 or less
50+	104+	84–102	76–82	74 or less

What is your recovery pulse rate?

Recovery rate is an essential part of your fitness assessment. You should assess it before you start your exercise programme and use it as a test to see how far you have progressed on the road to fitness.

The Step Test for Recovery Pulse

There is a simple test which you can perform yourself. Breathe normally throughout.

1. Stand 30 cm (12 inches) away from a step or bench that is 20–25 cm (8–10 inches) high.
2. Keep your back straight, abdominal muscles in, and chest lifted.
3. Place both hands on your hips.
4. Take a step up on the bench. Place your heel down first, then the ball of the foot. Do not lean forward. Keep your body straight.
5. Step up and down (right foot up, left up, right down, left down) as fast as you comfortably can for 3 minutes.
6. Sit down. Wait for 30 seconds. Now take your pulse.

If your recovery rate is poor or fair, consult your doctor and start with a beginners' menu. If your recovery is good or excellent, you can start at advanced level and move on rapidly. Reassess your recovery pulse rate at the end of every stage in your exercise programme and chart its improvement.

The following chart shows what your recovery pulse rate should be 30 seconds after stopping exercise.

A word of caution

If you feel breathless, nauseous or dizzy during the test, stop immediately. Consult a doctor.

RPR: Men				
Age	*Poor*	*Fair*	*Good*	*Excellent*
20–29	102+	86–100	76–84	74 or less
30–39	102+	88–100	80–86	78 or less
40–49	106+	90–104	82–88	80 or less
50+	106+	92–104	84–90	82 or less

RPR: Women				
Age	*Poor*	*Fair*	*Good*	*Excellent*
20–29	112+	94–110	88–92	86 or less
30–39	114+	96–112	88–94	86 or less
40–49	116+	96–114	90–94	88 or less
50+	118+	100–116	92–98	90 or less

What is your basal metabolic rate?

The rate at which the body burns calories while at complete rest (lying down but not sleeping) over a 24-hour period is known as the basal metabolic rate (BMR). This implies the number of calories consumed by the body while at rest.

Metabolism includes two functions, and your BMR includes both:

- Anabolism or building up
- Catabolism or breaking down

These two processes go on simultaneously in the body, and a balance is maintained between the two.

Your BMR is a measure of your ability to utilize or burn up your caloric intake. A high BMR signifies that the food you eat is being rapidly utilized and consumed by the body for the purpose of generating energy. Conversely, a low BMR means that the food that you eat is not being utilized as rapidly, so the excess is stored as fat.

There are some people who have a high BMR so that they can eat their fill and never gain an ounce. Those with a low BMR are scared to eat even a morsel extra, for it will promptly be converted to fat and appear on their body.

It is difficult to calculate the BMR as a precise figure. However, this is not strictly necessary. Most people have an idea of whether their BMR is high or not. What is important is to know the ways to improve your BMR so as to get the maximum benefit from your diet and exercise programme.

- The BMR decreases with age. A man of 40 cannot eat as he did at 20 without putting on weight. Food requirements decrease with advancing age, for the BMR slows down, and less food is enough to sustain the body.
- The BMR decreases in individuals who are on a very low calorie diet, or who are starving. People who go on hunger strikes for prolonged periods often do not lose weight. They lose muscle mass and energy, but their weight remains constant. This is why starvation is not a good way to lose weight.
- Exercise is one of the best ways to boost the BMR. Exercise not only raises the BMR, it also maintains it at a high level for some time. Early morning exercise is considered beneficial as you will not only burn calories while you are working out, but the high BMR means that you will continue to burn calories well into the day and any food consumed will be rapidly metabolized.
- Genetics has a role to play in deciding your BMR. Children of rapid metabolizers often have a good BMR themselves. This, and food habits, together explain why obese parents have obese children, while the offspring of lean and thin individuals are themselves slim and trim.
- Certain diseases alter your metabolism to such a degree that you begin to lose or gain weight, despite unchanged diet and exercise patterns. A common example is diseases of the thyroid gland. The sole function of the thyroid is to regulate metabolism. When this gland produces less amounts of the hormone thyroxine—a condition known as hypothyroidism—it leads to lethargy, weight gain,

decreased appetite, constipation, and even depression and memory loss. Conversely, persons who have excess of thyroxine—a condition known as hyperthyroidism—appear to be hyperactive, with twitching muscles, rapid pulse, palpitations and loss of weight.

How good is your overall sense of well-being?

Your overall feeling of health and well-being is a very good guide to fitness. Fit people usually are healthy and take pleasure in their day-to-day life experiences. Each day is a celebration of life.

Try this simple quiz to see how fit you are. Tick if the answer is yes:

- ☐ **Do you have disturbed sleeping habits?**
- ☐ **Are you habitually irritable and bad tempered?**
- ☐ **Do people joke about your bulging belly?**
- ☐ **Do you hold the banister to yank yourself up the stairs?**
- ☐ **Do you feel breathless after climbing two flights of stairs rapidly?**
- ☐ **Do you routinely skip meals?**
- ☐ **Are you chronically disgruntled with your job, spouse or peers?**
- ☐ **Do spend hours lolling in front of the TV?**
- ☐ **Are you in the habit of brooding over past wrongs for days on end?**
- ☐ **Are you a habitual worrier?**
- ☐ **Are you addicted to alcohol, nicotine, cocaine, tranquillizers or hallucinatory drugs?**
- ☐ **Have you been in and out of hospitals several times in the past year for minor or major problems ?**
- ☐ **Do you have high-calorie snacks (burgers, chips, aereated drinks) more than occasionally?**
- ☐ **Have you been fired from your job more than once?**
- ☐ **If the nearest market is about half a mile away, would you prefer to drive rather than walk?**

If you have ticked

Only 1 or 2 of the above, you are in fairly good shape.

3–5 of the above, your fitness levels leave a lot to be desired. You are physically not up to the mark and you are stressed. You need to exercise regularly and build up stamina, and try to solve the mental and emotional problems facing you.

More than 6 of the above, watch out! You are under a great amount of mental stress and are totally out of shape. Do not neglect yourself.

What is the state of your mind?

Diseases of the mind effect the body, and vice versa. That is why your mind plays an important role in your level of fitness.

Many patients who suffer from chronic illnesses or pain, such as cancers or heart problems, often develop some kind of mental problem—such as anxiety, depression, insomnia and phobias—as a direct result of prolonged bodily illness. Those who are obese also sometimes have to put up with social ridicule, which may cause anger, resentment, shame, guilt and depression.

Mental or emotional stress may lead to diseases of the body. Bronchial asthma, hypertension, skin disorders and heart problems are some conditions where the mind has an important role to play in the genesis of disease. Such diseases are known as psychosomatic disorders.

Apart from vigorous physical exercise, you can create a change in your state of mind through meditation, yoga, spirituality or positive thinking, whatever you find suitable.

Starting an Exercise Programme

Before you start on an exercise regime, you need to tailor one to your individual needs and also plan how exactly you are going to set about working out. As with many other activities, half the battle lies in the planning.

1. Make a medical record card for yourself.

1. **Name** ....
2. **Age** ....
3. **Sex** ....
4. **Weight** ....
5. **BMI** ....
6. **Waist circumference** ....
7. **Waist-hip ratio** ....
8. **RPR** ....
9. **Recovery pulse rate** ....
10. **History of illness** ....
    - **Pulmonary tuberculosis** ....
    - **High blood pressure** ....
    - **Diabetes** ....
    - **Bronchial asthma** ....
    - **Allergies** ....
    - **Heart disease** ....
    - **Chronic or acute back problems** ....
    - **Any joint injuries** ....
    - **Chronic fever** ....

- **Any surgery ....**
- **Hernia (operated or unoperated) ....**
- **Any fracture or dislocation ....**

11. Present or past gynaecological problems (For women only) ....

- **Heavy bleeding ....**
- **Discharge ....**
- **Pelvic pain ....**
- **Any cyst or tumour in the uterus or ovaries ....**
- **Number of children (Normal delivery or Caesarians) ...**

12. Any significant family history of illness ....

13. Investigations done recently ....

14. Investigations done in the past ....

15. Doctor's prescriptions ....

16. Any other information you think is relevant ....

Filling out your medical card will give you a clear picture of what are the risk factors, if any, which you should keep in mind.

- If you have a past history or present problem with any of the diseases listed, you should consult a doctor. You may require certain specific laboratory tests depending on your history and examination which your doctor may recommend.
- If you are over the age of 35, you should have a medical check up done before you start or intensify an exercise programme.
- If you are over 40, you should get an ECG performed. Your cardiologist might recommend a stress test.
- If you have a history of obesity, you should consult a doctor to conduct an exercise tolerance test before starting.
- If you have any hesitation or doubt in your mind, consult your doctor.

Some gyms require a fitness certificate or conduct their own tests.

2. Remember some important rules of exercising

It is important that you are aware of the nine rules of safe exercising before you start any programme. You must always remember these.

- **Take it slow**: Start at a comfortable low level; increase exertion very gradually. If you are unaccustomed to any form of exercise, you can start from as little as 5 minutes a day, and increase it by 3–5 minutes every couple of days until you have reached 20 minutes.

  Begin gradually, perhaps with brisk walking. Always exercise at a brisk but comfortable pace. Your breathing should be harder and faster than normal but you should be able to carry on a conversation while you are exercising.

The myth of sweating

Is it necessary to 'work up a good sweat'? No, say the experts. Sweating occurs more in humid surrounding, where evaporation of sweat from the skin decreases as a result of the high moisture content of the atmosphere. In such conditions, you may be sweating even though your work out is not adequate. Conversely, if the atmosphere is dry, sweat is rapidly absorbed from the skin and you feel cool. Ultimately, the pulse rate is the best guide to monitor your exercise.

Don't expect to get into shape overnight. Your fitness should start to improve within three months with consistent effort.

- **Know your limits**: If you are excessively fatigued, having persistent soreness or aches, you are probably doing too much.

  However, a little bit of muscular pain is to be expected whenever you start on any exercise programme especially during the first week. This should not be a deterrent to exercise.

- **Be regular**: Daily exercise is the optimum; but often hard to achieve. Aim for at least three or four workouts every week, each lasting at least 20 minutes. Five or six workouts is satisfactory.

Do not skip exercise for trivial reasons. Stop if you become ill, or on your doctor's advice. It can take many weeks, even months, to reach peak conditioning. But your fitness levels can be lost in a week or two of inactivity.

- **Warm up first**: It is important to prepare the body for exercise. A sudden onslaught of unaccustomed effort can precipitate muscle and joint injuries. Stretching exercises, done prior to a workout, condition the muscles for further effort. The older you are, the more important it is to protect the heart. Strenuous exercise, more so if performed after a gap of several days, can lead to a sudden and dangerous rise in the blood pressure and can damage the heart itself, which cannot cope with the increased demands of the body. Warming up prevents stiffness of the muscles, prevents post-exercise pain and soreness, and prepares the heart and lungs for extra effort.
- **Start easy**: You cannot do cross-country running or high-impact aerobics on the first day. Easy exercises are those that cannot harm the body. Certain types of physical activities are easy on the body, such as swimming and pool exercises, where water acts as a buffer to prevent muscle and joint trauma. Walking at an easy pace and cycling are other aerobic exercises that can be started anywhere, anytime, and you can regulate the duration and intensity of the exercise. These are least likely to be harmful. Cardiac patients, asthmatics, pregnant women and the elderly should start with these, and only when the body, muscles, joints and especially the heart have attained some degree of conditioning should they progress to more strenuous and complicated exercise.
- **Stay hydrated**: It is a myth that you should not drink water during exercise. Exercise causes the body to lose large amounts of water in the form of sweat. Sports persons, when weighed before and after a bout of exercise, have been found to weigh almost 1 kilogram less; this is due to water loss and can lead to severe dehydration. It is a good idea to take small sips of water during exercise. Thirst is a late sign of dehydration and occurs when the body has been left craving for water for a long time.

- **Do not fast**: It is a myth that one should exercise on an empty stomach. Severe or sustained effort, made in the fasting state, can cause blood sugar to fall rapidly, and if sufficient body reserves have not been mobilized in time, the result can be a hypoglycemic or 'low blood sugar' attack, leading to dizziness, nausea and fainting.
- **Cool off slowly**: The body needs time to get back to its resting state; this includes muscles, joints, heart and lungs. Never stop vigorous exercise abruptly. Walk for at least 2–5 minutes after a jog or brisk workout, and decelerate gradually while you are walking. Breathe deeply during the cool off phase. Take a warm shower rather than a very hot or cold one. Stretching exercises that promote flexibility should be added to each session.
- **Do not ignore warning signs**: Be alert to any evidence of tissue damage or injury. Any sudden acute pain in the back or knees, or any persistent stiffness or soreness in any part of the body is a signal for you to stop exercise immediately. Pain in the chest or radiating to the back, neck or arms, with or without sweating, palpitations and breathlessness, could be a sign of an incipient heart attack. Consult your doctor immediately. If you feel chest pressure, dizziness, weakness, nausea, or unexpected shortness of breath, stop exercising and relax. If the symptoms persist, seek medical help.

3. Define your goals

Before you start on your workouts, you should know what you are aiming for. Do you simply want to lose weight? Are you aiming for a lean, muscular body? Do you want to develop strong and bulky muscles? Are you looking for strength and stamina? Of course working out will do all these things, but depending on your priority, you must choose your exercises. Otherwise exercise can be counterproductive to your goal.

Only when you have defined your goals should you start on an exercise programme. Discuss your objectives with your gym instructor or personal trainer. The results of your exercise sessions depend largely on your commitment to exercise, and the ability to stay focussed on your goals.

Your workout plan depends on what you want to achieve.

STRENGTH, STAMINA, AND FLEXIBILITY			
	Strength	*Stamina*	*Flexibility*
Cycling	✓✓	✓✓✓	✓
Dancing		✓	✓✓✓
Football	✓✓	✓✓	✓✓
Golf			✓
Gymnastics	✓✓	✓	✓✓
Hill walking	✓	✓✓	
Jogging	✓	✓✓✓	✓
Judo	✓	✓	✓✓✓
Racquet sports (Tennis, badminton)	✓	✓	✓✓
Rowing	✓✓✓	✓✓✓	✓
Squash	✓	✓✓	✓✓
Swimming	✓✓✓	✓✓✓	✓✓✓
Walking		✓	
Weightlifting	✓✓✓		
Yoga			✓✓✓

✓ Beneficial effect ✓✓ Very good effect ✓✓✓ Excellent effect

4. Make a workout plan

Once you know what you are aiming for, you should read up on that target or talk to your trainer or gym instructor to find out what exercises are most suitable for you. You also need to decide whether you are going to work out at home, in a gym or undertake outdoor activities like running or cycling.

What your target is will also determine how frequently you should exercise. For example, if weight loss is your goal, then it is imperative

YOUR GOAL AND YOUR WORKOUT

Goal	*Activities*	*Notes*
Endurance training	Cycling, rowing, running or stair-climbing done at a moderate to high level (70–80 per cent of maximum heart rate) for 45–60 minutes.	These allow for high intensity workouts that increase endurance levels.
Weight loss	Walking, jogging, swimming, cycling, dancing, rowing and skipping can all be weight-loss activities, if done at a moderate to high intensity level for at least 20 minutes.	Any exercise that you do will consume calories. More calories are burnt in aerobic exercise as compared to, say, stretching.
Muscle definition	Choose a circuit of exercises with minimal rest (30 seconds) between sets, i.e. do weight training with rapid shifts from exercise to exercise.	This results in substantial increase in caloric expenditure, ultimately helping you to decrease body fat and heighten definition.
Muscle building	You require workouts with heavy weights. This will build muscles, but remember to follow a low-volume, high-intensity workout. This is best done under supervision. You may combine this with aerobic activities where you train at roughly 60–80 per cent of your maximum heart rate: cycling, running, stair-climbing, or rowing for at least 20 minutes. Another option is to use circuit/aerobic weight training on your 'light' days to improve cardiac health and increases caloric expenditure.	Some body builders feel that aerobic activity 'takes away' from muscle building. They focus only on strength training, combined with a high protein diet.

that you work out every day. On the other hand, if you are working on bodybuilding, having a split routine makes sense.

It is good to chalk out your own exercise plan depending on what your needs are. You can model it on the 20-minute exercise programmes given in the next section. You may need to periodically modify your target depending on what you have achieved in the intervening period.

The key to weight loss is 'gradual and sustained'. Ideally you should not lose too much weight suddenly. A weight loss of about 500 grams per week is within safety limits and beneficial. It increases the odds of keeping weight off for a long time because of the healthy behaviour patterns you have developed. In addition, the weight loss tends to be primarily fat, with little loss of muscle mass.

If you are losing more weight per week, this suggests that you are exercising too vigorously and not balancing it by an adequate intake. This kind of accelerated weight loss is undesirable and should not be attempted. You are probably not only losing fat, but muscle mass as well.

It is important that you select activities that you enjoy and that you include a variety to prevent boredom and to involve more muscles.

5. Plan your schedule

Decide when, where, how often and with whom you will work out.

A word of caution

There is no such thing as spot reducing—losing inches in one particular area of the body where you have accumulated fat. Spot reducing is not possible because calories are taken from fat stores throughout the body, not just from the area being exercised.

The amount you lose in any given area depends on how much is there in the first place. If you tend to put fat on the hips more than any other area, you will lose more fat from the hips. When you exercise a particular area of the body, the underlying muscle becomes more firm and may give the appearance of decreased weight, but the changes are related to muscle development.

Seek support from your friends and family, and believe that you can succeed. Having a positive mindset is vital.

Few people lose weight without occasional periods of discouragement and frustration. You may reach plateaus where there seems to be no progress. It is important to have a positive attitude during periods like that. Some people benefit from the motivation provided by weight-loss support groups. You can find one in your city or form your own support group with like-minded people with common goals.

If you are planning to exercise out of doors, have a back-up plan for bad weather.

An important part of planning your schedule is to decide when to exercise. Scientists have long debated the question of when it is most beneficial to exercise. For many people, the time when you exercise is determined by your daily schedule.

Much research has been done to link the body's circadian rhythms (the daily cycles that regulate body temperature, metabolism and blood pressure) with exercise to determine what time of day exercise is most effective. It is generally concluded that when your body temperature is high, your workout will be more effective than if you exercise when your body temperature is low. Generally, body temperature dips to its lowest point about 1–3 hours before you wake up. It reaches its peak late in the afternoon. Thus, it would be safe to assume that your workouts will be more effective in the late afternoon. The muscles are warm, your strength is at an all-time high, and your resting pulse rate and blood pressure are low.

However, what is actually important is that you do exercise regularly, so you should just do it whenever it is convenient and when you will not forget to do it. It depends on two factors:

- What exactly is your schedule? Are you too busy in the late afternoon or evening to exercise? Will mornings work better for you? Or will you have to alternate between morning and late noon or evening workouts?

- When do you feel your best? Everyone has one particular time of the day when he or she feels full of energy, at peak form, and that is the time that should be kept aside for exercise. If you are not a morning person, you might perform better at the end of the day when you are wide awake. There is no point dragging oneself out of bed early in the morning to do a few half-hearted exercises. Does your energy flag by the end of the day? If that is so, exercise will be the last thing on your mind. Because you're exhausted, you will not exercise to your fullest potential.

Traditionally early morning is the time considered best for exercise. You are free from other commitments. You feel more alive and willing to exercise. You still have the whole day in front of you and you have that much more energy to tackle activities. You don't have to contend with scheduling problems that often occur later in the day. There aren't many other distractions to prevent you from exercising. If you are new to exercise, consider committing to mornings to increase your adherence to your new routine. Studies have shown that people who exercise in the morning are more likely to stick with their exercise programmes.

There is one exception to choosing a time that suits you best. If you are training for an athletic event like a marathon or a race or a regatta, exercise at the time the event will take place. For example, if a cycling event starts at 8 a.m., get used to cycling at that time, especially if you are used to working out later in the day. This will help your body adjust to the demands of the event.

For morning exercisers

1. **Lay your clothing out the night before. When your alarm rings, you will be able to leap into action without having to hunt for shoes and clothes and tennis racquets, or whatever it is that you need.**
2. **Set two different alarms. If you simply love those extra 10 minutes in bed, set two different alarms, one by your bed and the other across the room. You will have to jump out of bed.**
3. **Exercise is always more fun with a partner. If you are ever tempted to miss your workout, your buddy will keep you going.**

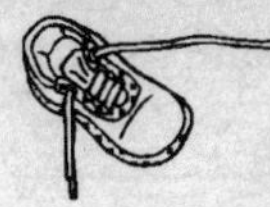

If you oversleep, your friend will be on the telephone, or better still, your doorstep.

For late afternoon/evening exercisers

1. **Set your exercise time and stick to it. Don't let other distractions tempt you to neglect your exercise programme. Small adjustments are okay, but try not to stray too far away from your goals. Remember, partying is better after a workout, not before. You will find it impossible to give your fullest if your stomach is loaded with food and drinks and your mind is heavy with sleep. Plan for eventualities such as traffic snarls.**
2. **If you are exercising outdoors, pay attention to the soaring temperatures and high humidity of summer. Your body will drag in the hot weather. You will also need to make certain you are well-hydrated in hot weather; drink more water than usual if you have been sipping on coffee or soft drinks all day.**

You also need to plan your gear and equipment. These are discussed in later chapters.

6. Monitor Yourself

- Attach an exercise log to your refrigerator and record each session. You will find a sample log in the next section.
- In order to exercise safely, you should constantly monitor the state of your body and be aware of warning signs. Your heart rate is your best guide in this matter. To ensure that you are working at the correct level of intensity, you need to monitor your heart rate before, during and after exercise.
- You should be aware of your RPR before you start exercising.
- You also need to calculate your target pulse rate (TPR).

While in theory, you could work at any intensity, in practice there are limits beyond which you should not push your heart. TPR is the pulse rate at which you should exercise. It is different from maximum heart rate. Your maximum heart rate is judged to be about 220 minus your age (in years).

During your workout, your pulse should be 60–80 per cent of your maximum heart. This is your TPR. You should try to sustain this for about 20 minutes. Do not exceed this rate.

> If you are 30, your maximum heart rate should be 220–30=190.
> During warm-up, your pulse rate should be 40–50 per cent of 190=76–95.
> During the workout, your pulse rate should be 60–80 per cent of 190 = 114–152. This is your TPR.

7. Make it fun

If you are a reluctant exerciser, then the word 'exercise' may conjure up visions of sweaty bodies and monotonous, endlessly repeated body movements that are both exhausting and uninspiring. But this need not be so. Regular exercise can be fun and invigorating.

- Find friends. Many people enjoy exercise more and find it easier to do regularly in the company of others. Get together with a friend or join a group that walks, rides bikes or goes to a gym.
- If you prefer to exercise at home, invest in equipment like a stationary bicycle or treadmill, and keep it in a convenient place. Listening to music or watching TV while you exercise can add enjoyment.
- Variety is the lifeline of fitness training. Do not allow yourself to get bored. Adding change to your exercise schedule not only prevents boredom, it also prevents muscle fatigue, for when you change over to another exercise, you are using a different set of muscles.
- Involve your family.
- Give yourself rewards. Plan treats for yourself: if you exercise regularly for two weeks, you will treat yourself to a movie; two months, and a new dress.
- Make exercise sessions lively and fun-filled. Wear suitable but smart clothes that make you feel good. Fill the house with laughter and music. Exercise sessions should resemble a picnic, not a military drill.

Aerobic exercises

Broadly speaking, exercises can be of two types: aerobic and anaerobic.

What are aerobic exercises?

Aerobic exercises are those that require a steady supply of oxygen, and in large quantities most of the time, to sustain the energy-giving powers of muscles. These exercises, naturally, strengthen the cardiovascular system and the respiratory system which are responsible for the intake and transportation of oxygen to the various parts of the body. The total circulating blood volume also increases. Another indirect benefit is an imperceptible rise in the haemoglobin content of the blood, which itself contributes to an increase in the circulating oxygen. The muscles of the heart and lungs grow stronger, the resting pulse rate is lowered, and the lung capacity increases.

An aerobic exercise is any continuous activity performed for a minimum of 20 minutes while maintaining a heart rate between 70–80 per cent of maximum heart rate and with the chief energy sources being oxygen and body fat.

Examples of aerobic exercises are walking, running, jogging, swimming, rowing, rope skipping and cycling. Dances of various kinds can also be aerobic exercise. Most racquet sports, like badminton, tennis and squash, also provide a good cardiovascular workout, and are considered aerobic exercises.

In order to strengthen your heart and lungs, aerobic exercises need to be sustained. Each workout should last for at least 20 minutes, and preferably more.

Aerobic exercises can be great fun. Enjoyment adds to compliance. Who can deny the pleasures of dancing? Tennis and badminton and squash can be played with friends, and competition adds to the fun. Walking and jogging could very well be a family affair.

Do all aerobic exercises have the same effects?

The answer is no. Theoretically, all the above mentioned exercises have been grouped together in one category. But each activity produces different results, at least as far as the muscles are concerned. While all aerobic exercises improve heart and lung functions and burn calories, the muscles used during different exercises can produce different results. The proof of this lies in the fact that body types vary according to the type of athletic activity chosen. Runners have lean, sinewy legs. Cyclists have strong, well-developed calf muscles and thighs. The strength, endurance and even the anatomy of muscles is defined by the activity you engage in.

It is therefore important to decide what your fitness goal is. Is it burning calories and improving cardiovascular fitness? If that is so, you can choose any aerobic activity that suits you. But if your goal is also a specifically defined figure, you need to be very careful in your choice. You may be engaging in an aerobic activity that is counterproductive to your goal.

In order to know the aerobic exercises most suited for your purpose,

- You should be aware of the different muscle groups and which ones are used during different activities.
- You should decide between high-resistance and low-resistance exercises.

What are the muscle groups?

Technical name	Where they are
biceps	front of arm
brachialis	front of upper arm, forearms
triceps	back of arm
deltoids	shoulder
sternocliedomastiod	neck
trapezius	upper back
pectorals	chest
intercostal	between the ribs
erector spinae	lower and middle back
paraspinal	back muscles
latissimus dorsi	back
obliques	sides of trunk
rectus abdominis (abdominals)	front of abdomen
gluteus maximus (gluteals)	buttocks
adductors	inner thighs
hamstrings	back of thighs
sartorius	inner thighs
quadriceps femoris (quadriceps)	front of thigh
rector femoris	along front thigh
gastrocnemius	back of calf
soleus	back of lower calf (combines with gastrocnemius to form the Achilles tendon)

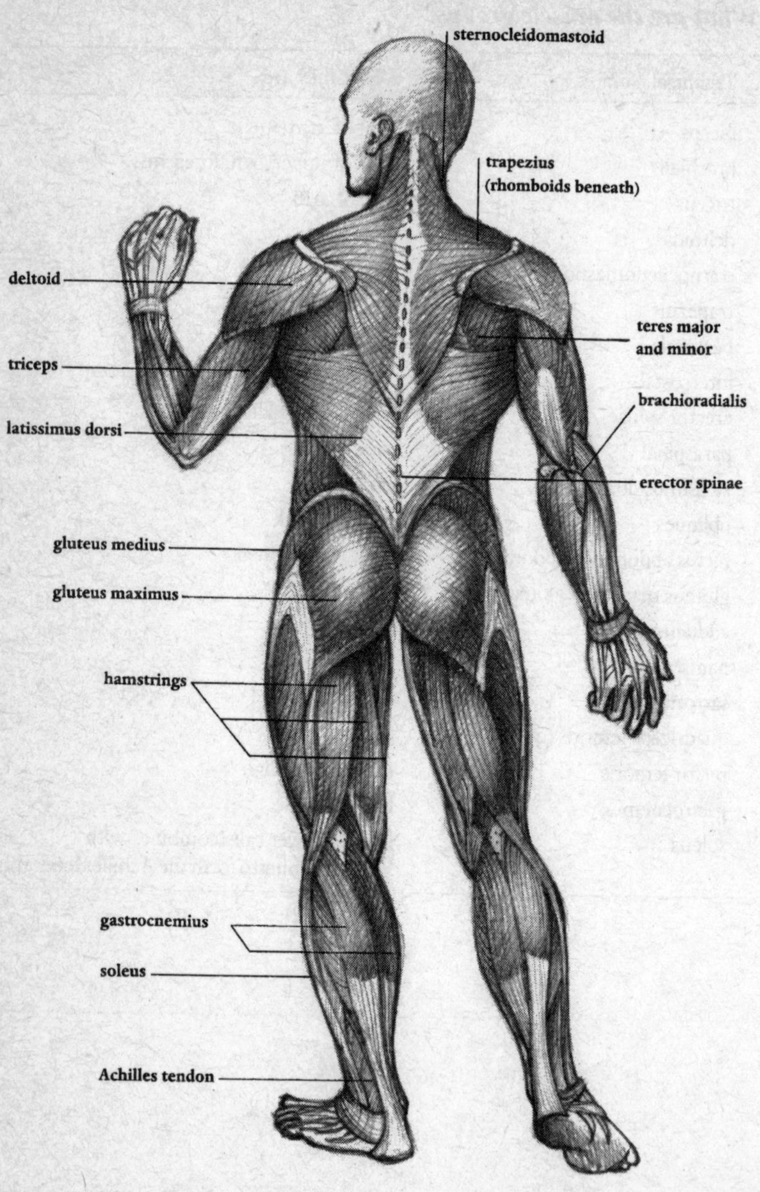
sternocleidomastoid
trapezius
(rhomboids beneath)
deltoid
teres major
and minor
triceps
brachioradialis
latissimus dorsi
erector spinae
gluteus medius
gluteus maximus
hamstrings
gastrocnemius
soleus
Achilles tendon

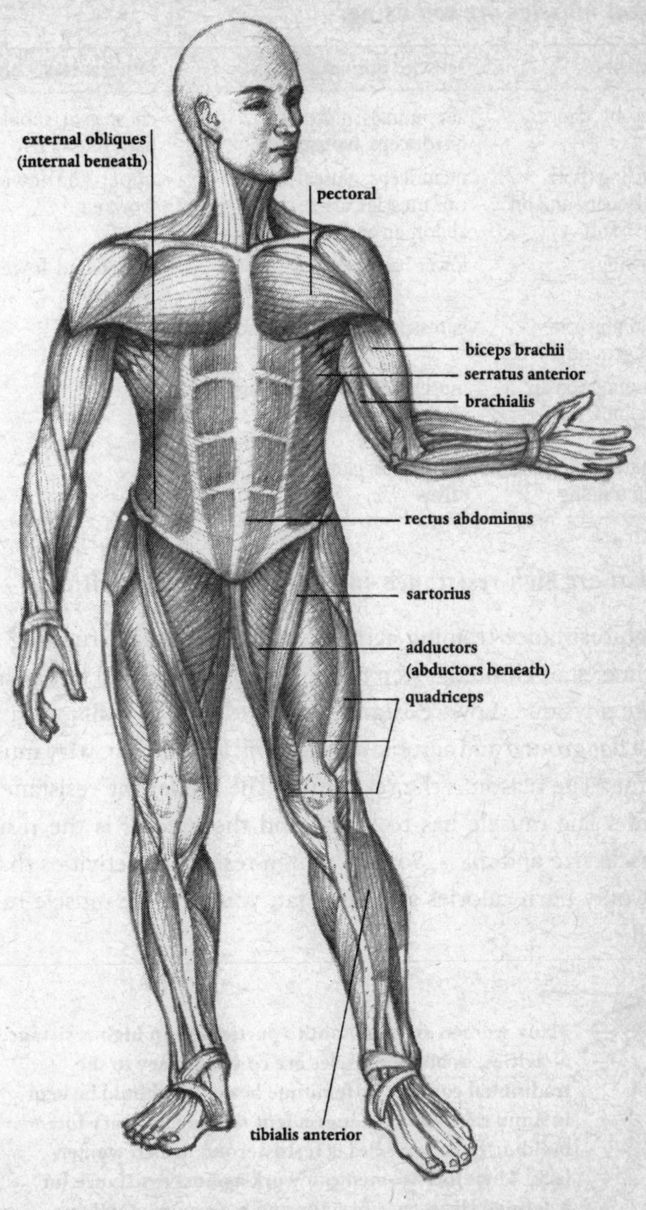
external obliques
(internal beneath)
pectoral
biceps brachii
serratus anterior
brachialis
rectus abdominus
sartorius
adductors
(abductors beneath)
quadriceps
tibialis anterior

What muscles are you using?

Activity	Muscles primarily used	Other muscles also used
Aerobic dance	abdominals, gluteals, quadriceps, hamstrings	chest, arm, shoulder and back muscles
Cycling (both stationary and on the road)	quadriceps, gluteal and calf muscles, arms, shoulders, abdomen and paraspinae	upper and lower body workout
Rowing	lower back muscles	upper and lower body workout
Running (on flat ground)	hamstrings and calf muscles	
Running (on an incline)	muscles of the lower trunk, gluteals, quadriceps and calf muscles	
Stair climbing and step training	quadriceps, gluteals and calves	

What are high-resistance and low-resistance activities?

High-resistance training activities, such as rowing, running on an incline, stair climbing, step training and cycling lead to a relatively large physique. Low-resistance activities such as walking, running on a flat ground and aerobic dancing will lead to thin, wiry muscular frame. The reason is the resistance. The higher the resistance, the harder the muscle has to work, and the greater is the resultant muscle size and mass. So it is in high-resistance activities that you not only burn calories and burn fat, you increase muscle mass as well.

Many women are reluctant to participate in high-resistance activities, as bulky muscles are contradictory to the traditional concept of feminine beauty. It should be kept in mind that one vital ingredient that is necessary for building bulky muscles is testosterone, which women lack. Therefore women can work against resistance for a defined clean-cut physique and maximum stamina and endurance.

Simple aerobic exercises

Walking

Walking is one of the best and simplest forms of aerobic exercise. A regular walking regime facilitates recovery from many ailments, including heart attacks. A brisk walk will relax you, and at the same time it will stimulate your thoughts.

- It has tremendous cardiovascular benefits.
- Calf muscles are so important to circulation that they are called the secondary pump, and their pumping action is considered second only to the heart. With every step you take, the calf muscles contract, and large amounts of blood are squeezed back into circulation.
- It has a morale boosting effect.
- It does not require any specific or expensive equipment, and can be done anywhere, anytime.
- It is good for beginners and athletes alike.
- It can be safely prescribed to those who have a low exercise tolerance.
- It does not put any strain on the joints and muscles. Chances of soft tissue or bone injuries are least for walkers.
- Heart patients, pregnant women, and patients of osteoarthritis, osteoporosis, tuberculosis, asthma and a host of other disorders can all benefit by walking. This includes those in whom vigorous exercise is contraindicated.

What is the right technique?

- Wear proper shoes. The right pair of shoes makes walking a joy; the wrong pair leads to sheer torture. Shoes should be neither too heavy nor too stiff, and should be of such a size that they fit comfortably even after the feet have started swelling up as a result of the walk. (*See pp. 94–98.*)

- Select a walking track. It should preferably be one which does not injure the bones and joints, and for this reason, a soft mud track is better than a concrete surface.
- Begin by walking at a moderate pace for 5 minutes in order to warm up. It is important to warm up before you stretch. Never stretch cold muscles as you risk a muscle pull or tear, or could develop microtrauma in the muscle fibres. Warming up prepares the muscles for more intensive effort later on and prevents tissue trauma. Your body gets prepared to start burning fat in order to produce energy.

Usually, when we exercise, the body burns sugars for the first 15 minutes. It is only later that oxidation of fat becomes a reality. So there is no point in starting with peak effort, you will only tire yourself out, while the fat loss will be negligible.

- Do stretching exercises (*see p. 51*).
- Swing your arms naturally according to the body rhythm while walking.
- Start slowly. Build up speed gradually. Walk faster as you go. Do not force yourself to increase your stride unduly, this will put an unnecessary strain on the thigh muscles and can cause injury.
- Walk to attain your TPR (*see pp. 41–42*) and hold it for at least 20 minutes.
- Hold your head up high. Keep your back straight. Do not stoop.
- Bring your heel down first.
- For better coordination, try walking sideways and backwards.
- When you are drawing to the end of your walk, slow down. Walk at about half the intensity for 5 minutes to cool down. Do relaxing exercises.
- Check for visibility and safety if you are walking at night or

before daybreak. As far as possible, walk with a friend for extra encouragement and motivation.

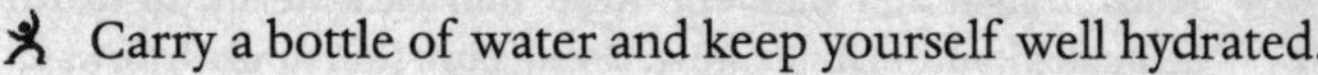

- Carry a bottle of water and keep yourself well hydrated.

Stretching exercises for walkers

Stretching adds flexibility, makes walking more comfortable, and allows you to gain more distance. You must do warm-up exercises before stretching.

***Head circles*: Make quarter circles with your head. Start with your ear near your shoulder on one side, rotate your head around to the front, going over to the opposite side. Roll your head back to the other side. Repeat five to ten times.**

***Arm circles*: Both backward and forward circles need to be done. With one arm at a time, make backwards arm circle with your palm facing out, thumb pointed up. Repeat ten to fifteen times with each arm. Then make forward arm circles with the palm facing in, thumb pointed down. Repeat ten to fifteen times.**

***Hip stretch*: Stand up, take a half-step back with the right foot. Bend your left knee and shift your weight back to your right hip. While keeping the right leg straight, bend forward and reach further down your right leg. Hold for 15–30 seconds. Change sides. Repeat 10 times.**

***Quadriceps stretch*: Stand erect, holding onto a wall for support. Bend your knee behind you so that you can grasp your foot, holding your heel against your butt. Stand up straight and push your knee gently back as far as you can, the hand just keeps the heel in place. You might find it more comfortable to use the hand from the opposite side. Hold for 15–30 seconds. Now repeat with the other leg. Repeat ten times on each side.**

***Calf stretch*: Stand an arm's length from the wall. Lean into wall, bracing yourself with your arms. Place one leg forward with knee bent—this leg will have no weight put on it. Keep other leg back with knee straight and heel down. Keeping back straight, move hips towards wall until you feel a stretch. Hold for 30 seconds. Relax. Repeat with other leg.**

***Achilles stretch*: From the calf stretch position, bend the back knee so that the angle is changed to stretch the Achilles tendon. Keep your heel down. Hold for 15–30 seconds.**

***Leg extensions*: Stand and hold the back of a chair. Bending at the knee, bring one leg forward, then extend and swing that leg back and behind. Repeat ten to fifteen times, then switch legs.**

The right posture

- **Walk straight and walk tall. Keep your back steady, so that it maintains its normal curvature. Do not push your stomach forward.**
- **Lift your head high. Keep your chin straight and parallel to the ground. Do not look down while walking. Focus your eyes 10 feet ahead on the road, not just in front. This way you can see the track and avoid injuries due to potholes or irregularities on the walking surface.**
- **Pull your butt in especially while taking deep breaths.**
- **Let your arms move naturally with the body's intrinsic rhythm while walking. They should be bent at 90° at the elbows, and move in a backward and forward direction. Swing arms opposite to the leg movement. Do not let your arms cross in front of your body or fling them about. Normal walking motion uses arms to counterbalance the leg motion. You can add power and speed just by using arms effectively.**
- **Do not slap the ground with each step. Do not walk flat-footed.**
- **Do not lean your body backward or forward.**
- **Do not increase your stride in an effort to gain extra ground. If speed is the aim, walk with quick small steps.**

Is outdoor walking better than walking on the treadmill?

This is a matter of personal choice. There are those who swear by early morning, outdoor walks, and there are those who believe that nothing can be better than jumping out of bed straight onto a treadmill.

The treadmill, or indoor walker, in its simplest form consists of a moving belt, the speed of which can be adjusted, on which a person is compelled to walk if he doesn't want to fall off. (*Treadmills are discussed in more detail in the chapter 'The Right Gear'*.) Newer machines are of highly sophisticated design. You can adjust not only the speed but also the incline of the walk, and simultaneously, the machine measures your heart rate, and calories burnt. The advantage of the treadmill is that you can walk unconcerned about the vagaries of the weather, and at a convenient time, in the comfort of your home or gym. You can calculate how much you have actually achieved and you are free of distractions. Walkers in a park or on a jogging track are often likely to slow down in order to meet friends and catch up on news, and speed is the first casualty.

But outdoor walking has its own pleasures. The sight of others walking can be an incentive, and what is more, the sight of an obese person struggling and sweating on a jogging track can make you stronger in your resolution to attain fitness. An early morning walk has other benefits, there is no smog and no smoke fumes, the air is pure, it is soothing to be amidst nature. The disadvantage of outdoor walking is that there is usually little or no control over the workout itself. After a while, one tends to lose speed without realizing it. This can easily be rectified by having the right approach and the right motivation, and of course a finger on the pulse. A pedometer is of immense use.

How often should you walk?

Beginners should start slowly. Start with a 5–10 minute walk, four to five times a week. Gradually increase the time spent in walking so as to increase your distance. You can increase your walking time by 10 per cent per week to a maximum of 1 hour a day. After that, work on increasing your speed. But there is no need to rush through things. Check your speed after weeks, not days.

Ideally, you should walk daily. If you have to miss a day or more, restart as soon as possible. Start at a speed and walk a distance that is less than your usual. Build up gradually. Skip a day if you feel soreness in your muscles or chronic tiredness.

What is the best speed?

Choose your own speed, at least when you start. Do not be guided by others. What suits others might be too strenuous or too slow for your liking. Let your pulse rate guide you in this matter. Try to attain your target heart rate, though not on the first day.

As a general rule, your speed should be such that you are breathing harder and faster, but not gasping for breath. You should be able to keep up a conversation as you walk. When starting on a walk routine, it is worthwhile to remember that distance is more important than speed. It is better, at least in the beginning, to increase the distance covered, and only when you are able to walk 20 kilometres a week should you attempt to gain speed.

Preventing heat stroke

- **Walk when it is cool. If you live near the seashore, keep track of sea breezes. If you live far from the coast, you should walk early in the morning or in the late afternoon, when the suns rays are at an incline, and therefore least intense.**
- **Hydrate yourself. Have half a litre of water before you start walking. Do not wait for thirst to set in, thirst is a late sign of dehydration and by the time you are thirsty your body cells are already depleted of water. Keep sipping 150–200 ml every half an hour.**
- **Wear loose cotton clothes, preferably long sleeved, of light colours, which reflect, rather than trap, the rays of the sun. You can buy walking clothes made of polypropelene, a fabric that sucks sweat away from the skin and allows for easy evaporation.**
- **Carry water. Sprinkle some on yourself if it gets really hot. Evaporation of water requires energy, and your body will have to surrender heat in order to evaporate water or sweat. This will have a cooling effect.**
- **Protect the back of your neck and head by a cotton scarf or a hat.**
- **Wear sunglasses, preferably wraparound ones. This prevents damage to the eyes by UV rays.**
- **Wear sunscreen with SPF of 15 or more to prevent sunburn and wrinkles.**

Walking in cold weather

- **Protect yourself. Wear adequate warm clothes over your usual walking gear. You should feel comfortable, not hot. Wear a waterproof and windproof jacket if required. It is better to wear several light layers than one heavy layer of woolen clothing. You can discard as you go along.**
- **Walk with the wind in your face. This way, you will have the wind in your back on your return which will make things easier when you are tired.**
- **Select a route that is safe from the wind. Trees afford good protection.**
- **Select areas free from ice and puddles.**
- **Check for visibility. Keep a torch handy.**

How many calories do you burn during walking?

Different textbooks give different figures. The reason is that the energy utilized is not simply a function of distance covered, it also depends a lot on the body weight. Heavy people burn more calories in walking. This is because it requires more effort to propel a heavier body than a lighter one. As a general rule, calories burnt during walking range from 150 to 250 per hour, depending on weight.

So where does speed come in? If you are compromising on distance covered because of a gain in the speed, you are aiming for cardiovascular fitness, but the total number of calories burnt may actually be less, as compared to walking at a slower pace. There are people who start walking at a terrific speed, only to flop down on the grass after a short distance. Here the actual number of calories burnt is very little. Then there are those who confuse perspiration with a good workout. If you walk very fast for a quarter of a mile and then stop because you are gasping and sweating, you may feel you have done your bit for the day. But the distance covered may not be very much. You have not lost much by way of calories either. It would be far better to walk at a relatively slower pace, but for a longer distance. Brisk walking is of use only if it is sustained.

What is power walking?

Power walking or speed walking is walking at such a speed and in such a manner as to give you a good cardiovascular workout. It is intense, fast walking with rapid arm pumping movements at a pace that is close to jogging. For this you need to improve technique, and if necessary, use weights for added benefit.

Power walking burns more calories, and this is not simply because you are covering more distance in the same time. It is also because power walking necessarily requires the use of other muscle fibres which are not usually used, and this extra consumption of energy by synergistic muscles helps you in losing more calories.

Speed has its own advantages. The catch is that the increase in speed should not mean decrease in the time spent in exercising, or in the distance covered. With power walking, the desired heart rate can be achieved easily.

For power walking good posture is a must. So is a stride that gives maximum efficiency and speed. Proper arm movements are required to give the necessary thrust to your attempt.

Power walking need not be a continuous, strenuous effort. If you find power walking difficult to sustain, start by alternating 1–2 minutes of power walking with 5–10 minutes of walking at a moderate pace. Gradually increase the time spent in power walking. For maximum benefit, do not decrease the distance covered.

Cross training

Cross training is the taking up of some other athletic activity, over and above what you normally do. Once adaptation to exercise occurs, the body no longer has to work very hard in order to accomplish what once may have been a difficult task, taking a lot of effort. Hence the value of cross training.

Those who power walk may need to work with weights, those who are into sprinting will benefit by something simple like water exercises. Change of form of exercise, intensity, duration and muscles used constitutes cross training.

Is walking with weights advisable?

Walking with weights is usually not considered advisable. It is sometimes done by those who walk with the specific aim of losing weight. The other two ways of achieving this are by increasing distance covered and time spent walking, and by power walking. However, walking with weights is more effective than these methods. The weights temporarily increase effective body weight, so you have to expend more energy to walk the same distance.

Some people try to increase the intensity of their walk by carrying weights in their hands or strapping weights to their ankles or wrists. This method is potentially harmful as the anatomy gets distorted, the biomechanics get thrown out of gear, and there is likelihood of getting a ligament pull, muscle sprain or strain.

A better method is to carry a backpack containing flat weights, such as 500 grams of books. Add a maximum of 500 grams every week until you are carrying a maximum weight of 5–7 kilograms. Do not carry more unless you have a personal trainer supervising every step.

Another safe method is to wear a weighted belt. Weight carried on the back or hips is borne by the strong trunk muscles, and there is minimal wear and tear, with less chance of injury.

Jogging

Jogging is the free movement of the body, at a rate slower than 15 kilometres per hour. At greater speeds, it is considered running.

The advantage of jogging over walking is that it burns more calories in the same period of time. It also leads to greater strength in the calf muscles and hamstrings, which become taut and more sharply defined. But jogging is also an exercise that requires extreme caution, for it makes a person prone to injuries. It has been reported that up to 50 per cent of all sports injuries are inflicted during jogging.

Jogging is meant for those who are in shape. A person who has been leading a sedentary lifestyle should not start jogging suddenly. It is not suitable for pregnant women or heart patients.

What is the right technique?

- Check with your doctor beforehand in case there are any medical problems.
- Wear proper shoes. (*Refer section on walking.*)
- Begin by warming up and stretching. (*Refer section on stretching for walkers.*)
- Run on a grassy field or soft track, where the 'give' of the track will prevent rebound injuries to the weight-bearing joints. Do

not run on surfaces that have no shock absorbing capacity, such as concrete.

- Run heel to toe. Bring the heel down first, and keep the toes pointing straight ahead.
- There is a lot of perspiration when jogging. Wear socks that absorb sweat. Stay hydrated.

What are the advantages of jogging on the treadmill?

Treadmill jogging is a useful alternative to outdoor jogging. Follow the instructions given for treadmill walking. Aim for a speed of 12–15 kilometres per hour. You can burn anything between 250 to 700 calories per hour while jogging, depending on your speed and your body weight.

How often should you jog?

Regular joggers can cover several miles a day if they are in peak condition. Beginners need to start very slowly as jogging can easily become exhausting. The best way to start jogging is to progress from walking to power walking, and then add brief spells of jogging. When you get tired, decrease speed and keep walking.

You can start with as little as a 30-second jog in a 10-minute walk. Gradually increase the time you jog, adding 30–60 seconds every two or three days. Intensify your efforts if you are comfortable. If your calf muscles feel sore or your knees hurt, stop jogging altogether, but continue to walk at a slower pace.

Is jogging with weights advisable?

The more you weigh, the more calories you burn while exercising. Jogging with weights is for those who are keen on losing weight in the shortest time possible. The disadvantage of this method is that the extra weight you carry puts a strain on the weight-bearing joints of the body. Unless you are careful, the hip, knee and ankles all can be adversely affected. Jogging with weights should only be done under supervision of a personal trainer. It is not recommended for pregnant women or patients with cardiac, respiratory or joint disorders.

(Also refer to the sections on preventing heatstroke and walking in the cold given earlier in the chapter.)

Cycling

Cycling is of aerobic benefit only if the speed is 20–25 kilometres per hour, or more. It has the added benefit that it is also a fast, efficient, non-polluting and cheap means of transport, and you can actually combine exercising with transport. Cycling puts less pressure on the bones and joints than jogging.

What are the benefits of cycling?

Apart from the general benefit of aerobic exercise—improved cardiovascular fitness—cycling also has specific benefits. It strengthens and builds the muscles of the upper and lower body, but especially the lower body (hamstrings, calf, gluteals and quadriceps).

However muscle hypertrophy is a direct consequence of work against resistance, so this will occur only in those cyclists who are committed, regular, and who pedal against resistance (up an incline, or with increased resistance on a stationary bike).

Gentle cycling can be done by all persons. But cycling is not recommended for patients with cardiac or respiratory problems or with hernias.

Any exercise that increases intra-abdominal pressure—such as weight training, isometric exercises and strenuous aerobic exercises—is contraindicated in hernia patients. Hernias are worsened by such attempts to exercise. Gentle walking or swimming is recommended instead.

What is the right technique?

- Choose a safe area, as far away from dust and pollution as possible.
- Wear a safety helmet
- Choose a cycle that is proportionate to your height. When seated, your feet should just touch the ground. Upright models of cycles let you sit erect, with head held high. Bent-over models of cycles are meant for speed, but they add to stress on your muscles.
- For added safety, choose a cycle with wide tyres with a good grip on the road.

Is outdoor cycling better than exercycles?

Stationary cycles, popularly known as exercycles, give all the benefits of cycling. (*Refer chapter 'The Right Gear' for more details.*) You do not need to worry about the vagaries of the weather, or the risks of traffic, or the problems of balance. Most stationary cycles come with built-in speedometers. You can increase your speed and your resistance each week. Some have handlebars that can move backwards and forwards to simulate a rowing motion, and these can be used to exercise the upper torso.

What is the best speed?

For aerobic benefit, your speed should be at least 16–20 kilometres per hour. Twenty-five kilometres per hour is a good speed for an average person to attain fitness. Greater speeds than this are only for those training for a race. The greater the speed, the more are the calories burnt, but the greater is the risk of accidents as control becomes poor at high speed.

How often should you cycle?

You can start with as little as 5 minutes per day of cycling. Gradually increase your times as you progress. For optimal results, you should be cycling for at least 20 minutes at a stretch, a minimum of three times a week.

How many calories do you burn while cycling?

This depends on your speed and weight.

At 15 kilometres per hour, you burn 300–600 calories, depending on your weight. At 25 kilometres per hour, you burn 500–900 calories.

(Also refer to the sections on preventing heatstroke and walking in cold weather given earlier in the chapter.)

Swimming and water exercises

Swimming is an aerobic exercise for the whole body. The buoyancy of water minimizes stress and helps prevent injuries. Swimming eases the pain of arthritis and decreases stiffness. It has been found that those persons who are unable to exercise due to severe joint disease are comfortable with slow swimming or water exercises.

What is the right technique?

- Follow rules and obey instructions of your swimming instructor, especially if you are a beginner or novice swimmer.
- Choose a swimming costume that is neither tight-fitting nor loose, and which allows free movement.
- Wear a swimming cap, and if required, a waterproof sunscreen.
- Never swim alone.
- Find a swimming pool that has lifeguards seated at vantage points along the length of the pool.
- Take time to build up stamina. Do not try swimming half a mile on your first day. Start with one or two lengths, then add a length each day as you go along.
- If you get cramps, do not panic. Float on your back. Let the affected limb relax. Use your other limbs to gently propel yourself to the edge of the pool.

- Do not indulge in any kind of horseplay while swimming.
- You should do a combination of swimming lengths and doing water exercises according to your specific needs.

What parts of the body are exercised?

Swimming tones and exercises the entire body, but specific muscle groups are exercised according to the stroke. The muscles which are exercised the most are the pectorals, triceps and latissimus dorsi.

How often should you swim?

You should ideally swim everyday, but if that is not possible, at least three times a week.

How many calories do you burn while swimming?

For aerobic benefit, you should swim at beat 10–15 metres per minute. The calories burnt depend on your speed and your weight.

Speed 15 metres per minute—you burn 250–450 calories per hour.

Speed 45 metres per minute—you burn 500–1000 calpries per hour.

What are the benefits of water exercises?

Exercising in water is much more easy and effective than making the same movements on land. The pull of gravity is minimized because of the upward thrust or buoyancy of water. This allows muscles, joints and ligaments to move with the minimum of stress. Water itself has a therapeutic effect, and water exercises can be done by persons of all ages, and of all degrees of fitness.

Though water exercises seem simple and easy, they are in fact more strenuous, for the simple reason that water has a certain amount of resistance, and in order to move in water one has to overcome this resistance. The same movement, when performed in water, will require at least 25 per cent more calories than on land. But while extra effort is required for water exercises, the water itself facilitates easy movements, making exercises seem less tedious and infinitely more gainful. Limbs become supple, stretching can be performed to a maximum without fear of injuries, and what is more important, water has a cooling effect, so you can exercise for longer periods of time without feeling fatigued.

It is best to exercise in chest-deep water, which should be neither too hot nor cold. If it seems a little chilly at first, it would be worthwhile to start with simple warming up exercises which condition the muscles and joints for further effort.

Warm-up and stretching exercises in water

Warm-up exercises should be done for 5–10 minutes. They can include the following:

- Knee lifting
- Holding the knee close to the chest and releasing slowly
- Raised leg stationary movement
- Walking at one point
- Walking on tiptoe
- Arm swings
- Twisting in one place
- Biceps curls—moving the forearm up and down in water

After warming up, you can do stretching exercises with forward, backward and sideward movements. Hold the stretched position for 6–10 seconds, then relax slowly.

You can improve your posture by water exercises. Stand straight with your back against the edge of the pool. Press against the pool wall and tighten buttocks. Pull in the abdominals. Hold for a few seconds, then relax.

Aerobic exercises for advanced levels

Circuit training

Circuit training is one of the best forms of aerobic exercise, but it is suitable for those at an advanced level. It is a full body workout that involves moving quickly from exercise to exercise. This fast-paced workout creates an aerobic effect by keeping your heart rate elevated. Any and all muscles can be used, depending on the exercises selected.

There are many kinds of circuit training, and you need to choose what best fits your goal, and train in an appropriate manner. The difference in training for endurance, weight loss, definition or muscle building lies in the level and length at which you train. For example, if you are trying to build your body, you need not run for an hour each day—this would be endurance training and would not help you to achieve a larger physique with prominent muscles. You should choose an activity that will move you closer to your fitness goals instead of doing a workout that might actually be sabotaging your plan.

After completing a circuit training workout, you will feel refreshed and less sore as circuit training promotes the removal of toxins which build up in the body during rigorous activity. During the deceleration periods in conventional methods, toxins become trapped within the tissues as the less active heart slows down the rate of blood flow. The continuous cardiovascular requirements of circuit training flush toxins out from the tissues by forcing the blood through the blood vessels, and your muscles recuperate faster because of the increased blood flow.

Can you get aerobic benefits while doing weight training?

Weight training has traditionally been considered an anaerobic activity. Some scientists believe that weight training lacks aerobic benefits, as it is not sustained and it does lead to an impressive build-up of muscles.

But it is also a scientifically proven fact that any form of exercise will stimulate the heart and lungs to maximum activity. Lifting weights does stimulate the heart and cardiovascular system to a certain extent.

If your goal is aerobic stamina with low body fat as well as anaerobic strength with impressive muscular shape—the good news is that weight training can be done aerobically through circuit training.

Conventional weightlifting methods recommend that each exercise set is followed by an adequate rest period. Thus the heart rate and blood pressure elevate during each exercise but dramatically reduce during rest intervals. This method involves plenty of non-active time to replenish ATP (and other anaerobic fuel), and to psyche-up for heavy weights. But the non-active time prevents the aerobic system from effective participation.

To get aerobic benefits from weight lifting, you have to perform one set with one exercise, then another without rest. Exercises can be sequenced in a variety of combinations which isolate single muscles, regional groups of muscles, or total body training. A simple way to do weight training aerobically would be to perform one set of weight training exercises, then do skipping, dancing or spot jogging in the rest period. If you can keep this up for 20 minutes, you have achieved a good cardiovascular workout.

If you are exercising in a crowded facility, or at home where you have to change equipment for every exercise (both time-consuming factors), aerobic benefits will be sacrificed when the body becomes less active. *Your mission is to stay moving.* Try doing sit-ups or push-ups or use a skipping rope you are forced to stop.

Conventional weight training methods suggest that you should handle heavier weights after phases of rest. Inter-set rest periods of up to 6 minutes replenish the ability to lift more weight but, at the same time, can expose the lifter to possible injuries as extended rest periods cool the tissues. Over-emphasis on heavy resistance can place too much stress on the muscles, tendons and ligaments.

Circuit training is beneficial and it minimizes the risks of weight training. Because it is continuous, resistance automatically becomes substantially lighter. The reduction in total weight lifted is compensated for by keeping the muscles exercised (eliminating inter-set rest intervals). As you remain active, the muscles can work just as hard as during conventional methods, but you get additional benefits to the heart and lungs.

Even if you are using conventional methods of weight training, you could try using circuit training at least once. This will break the monotony of heavy training, condition the heart and lungs, provide a mental challenge, and burn some extra fat. However, as long as you as you remain active during your workouts, you will accomplish everything you would normally achieve from an aerobics class, and you will also be taking advantage of specific muscle-shaping exercises.

The plateau effect

An oft-repeated lament is that though you may be exercising as much as before, you are no longer be losing weight! Many people find that after a point of time, the benefits of exercise, especially where it comes to weight loss, are no longer as apparent. The reason is that the body adapts to the changed conditions.

At this point, both intensity or duration must be increased in order to spark further improvements. You can increase intensity by increasing resistance, which is essentially weight training. Increasing duration can also help, but only in certain circumstances.

Researchers have found that changing the type of exercise, which leads to another group of muscles being involved, increases performance and results. So if you feel you have reached a plateau, simply increasing the duration of exercise will not help. You must switch over or add another exercise, preferably one with a higher resistance than before.

Anaerobic Exercise

Anaerobic exercises are high-intensity exercises that burn glycogen for instant energy, instead of using a steady supply of oxygen as provided by the cardiovascular and respiratory systems. The term anaerobic means 'without air' or 'without oxygen'. Anaerobic exercises create a temporary oxygen debt by consuming more oxygen than the body can supply. They use glycogen stored in muscles as the basic source of energy. During anaerobic exercises, muscles work at high intensity and a high rate of work for a short period of time. This helps to increase our strength and stay ready for quick bursts of speed. These exercises cannot last long because oxygen is not used for energy and a by-product, called lactic acid, is produced.

This also explains why a phase of recovery is essential between two bouts of anaerobic exercise. Lactic acid contributes to muscle fatigue and must be burned up by the body during the recovery period before another anaerobic bout of exercise can be attempted. The recovery period also allows the muscles to use oxygen to replenish the energy used during the high-intensity exercise.

Examples of anaerobic exercise include heavy weight lifting, sprinting, or any rapid burst of hard exercise. Think of hard and fast when you think of anaerobic activity. High-resistance anaerobic exercises are particularly useful for significantly improving muscular endurance, power and anaerobic capacity.

An ideal exercise programme will feature both aerobic and anaerobic activities

Again, the kinds of anaerobic exercises you choose to do depend on your fitness goals, and also your physical ability. The most important rule is to choose activities that you enjoy and that are accessible and feasible for you to do regularly.

There are four kinds of anaerobic exercise:

- Isotonic exercises
- Isometric exercises
- Calisthenics
- Isokinetic exercises

What are isotonic exercises?

Isotonic means 'same pressure'. These exercises are those whereby the muscle tone remains more or less the same, while the length of the muscle is altered during exercise. During these exercises, muscles contract against a resistance, and at the same time there is movement of a joint, such as in lifting a heavy weight. The most popular example is weight training.

What are isometric exercises?

Isometric means 'same length'. These exercises involve contracting muscles against other muscles or objects while keeping the length of the muscle unchanged (such as keeping your arm straight while squeezing a tennis ball). Pushing against a wall or statically flexing a muscle are examples of isometric contractions.

The key to this type of exercising is to hold the position for a period of time in order to induce muscle growth. By alternating muscle contractions for varied time periods, you can get a quick and easy workout.

During these exercises muscles contract against resistance without movement. Instead of building muscle mass, as in isotonic exercises, these exercises increase strength and tone without building bulk. To increase strength it is necessary to maintain a position in any one exercise for 6–8 seconds. The exercise should then be repeated five to eight times during each workout to ensure maximum muscular contraction.

Isometric exercises on their own are not recommended for strength training. They must only form part of a complete exercise programme.

If you suffer from heart disease or high blood pressure you should avoid isometric training. During muscular contractions in this form of exercise, blood pressure can rise alarmingly.

Isometric exercises are very useful in physiotherapy, where the aim is to improve muscle power. For example, patients of cervical spondylitis are taught neck isometrics, in order to strengthen the muscles of the head and neck. Isometric exercises are best taught by a qualified physiotherapist.

Contraction of muscles for a sustained amount of time increase heart rate. On a cardiovascular level, an increased heart rate will cause your body to burn more calories. Isometrics also lead to muscle failure (the soreness you feel after a workout), which itself will cause the body to burn calories for repairs. Additionally, repaired muscles become bigger and stronger, needing more calories for daily operations. Another side effect of this rebuilding process is the release of endorphins into the blood stream, which provide an invigorating sense of new-found energy as well as a release of tension.

What are calisthenics?

These are light exercises designed to promote general fitness, particularly useful for improving tone, endurance and flexibility of joints and muscles. These include stretching exercises, and exercises such as sit-ups, toe-touches, arm swinging, trunk twisting, push-ups, chin-ups and knee-bends, which help increase flexibility and joint mobility. Acrobatics, tai chi, some forms of yoga, and gymnastics are also calisthenics exercises. These are important for all, including competitive athletes. Such exercises are safe if done properly—with graduated increases in intensity, duration, resistance and number of repetitions. Calisthenics exercises usually do not expend sufficient energy to significantly reduce obesity, but are particularly useful as warm up and cool down exercises for those engaged in more vigorous activities.

What are isokinetic exercises?

Isokineic literally means 'same speed'. These are exercises performed with a specialized apparatus that provides variable resistance to a movement, so that no matter how much effort is exerted, the movement takes place at a constant speed. Such exercise is used to test and improve muscular strength and endurance, especially after injury. In such exercises, a weight is lifted through an entire range of motion. The goal is to see how much force can be applied at different movement speeds, which can only be done by the specialized apparatus.

In such exercises, the weight is not only being lifted. It is also being moved to a point and then pulled back to a starting point. These exercises increase both power and endurance.

What are the benefits of anaerobic exercise?

Anaerobic exercises are short term, and emphasize building muscle, rather than burning oxygen. Currently available medical data reinforces the importance of anaerobic exercise. While aerobic exercise is essential for cardio-respiratory fitness, all the other components of fitness—body composition, lean muscle mass, flexibility, muscular strength, coordination, agility and speed—are more easily attained through anaerobic exercise.

It is fallacious to think that only competitive athletes and sports persons require the fitness attributes that anaerobic exercises provide. Anaerobic exercises are necessary for one and all, irrespective of age and sex, not only to increase the lean body mass but also because they cause direct deposition of calcium in the bones, increase bone density and thus prevent osteoporosis. They also increase your strength and endurance.

Strength and Endurance

Strength is the ability to exert maximum force, either by a group of muscles or by a single muscle.

Endurance is the ability of a muscle or a group of muscles to exert force or overcome resistance continuously, for an extended period of time.

Lifting 30 kilograms for a few seconds is a matter of strength. Carrying a 30-kilogram load for half an hour is a matter of endurance.

What is anaerobic metabolism?

Anaerobic metabolism is one of the ways in which your body transforms 'fuel' from the food you eat into energy. Oxygen is supplied to the muscles indirectly, through stored carbohydrates, rather than directly, or aerobically, through the lungs. Anaerobic metabolism fuels short bursts of activity, when your body requires energy faster than the cardiovascular system can provide it aerobically. Carbohydrates (in the form of sugars called glucose and glycogen) store oxygen for immediate energy production in the body anaerobically. On the other hand, when energy demands are gradual and longer term, the body's aerobic metabolism handles the slower, steadier and direct form of oxygen supply to the muscles.

What is the anaerobic threshold?

Once your body switches from the short-term anaerobic metabolism to the longer-term aerobic metabolism, moderate levels of activity can be sustained by aerobic metabolism alone. However, if a sudden burst of energy is required (such as the last sprint at the end of a race), your body is again forced to produce the extra energy anaerobically. This metabolism switch is called the anaerobic threshold. Unfortunately, one of the byproducts of anaerobic metabolism is lactic acid, a harmful waste product that causes muscle pain and fatigue. The body requires additional oxygen to break down lactic acid, which is why you may gasp for air when you pass the anaerobic threshold. You are repaying your 'oxygen debt'.

How do anaerobic exercises improve endurance?

The body's stores of glucose and glycogen also fuel muscular endurance. One way to improve endurance is to increase the body's supply of carbohydrates. Dieticians recommend a diet where 60–80 per cent of daily calories come from complex carbohydrates. Such a diet can increase energy reserves in the muscles, prolonging the time before muscle fatigue takes place.

You can also improve endurance by gradually increasing the reps of a given movement and by following each set of reps by a rest period. This allows the body to eliminate excess lactic acid.

Activities that require energy faster than the cardiovascular system can provide are considered anaerobic.

To build muscle strength, steadily increase the weight that a muscle resists. To build endurance, increase the repetitions of an action.

Improving or maintaining health and an overall feeling of well-being should be a primary goal of an exercise programme. Resistance training, also known as weight training, can play an important role in the development of self-confidence and body satisfaction by increasing strength, building and toning muscles, and increasing muscular endurance. It can also help maintain lean body mass, which is very important for individuals attempting weight loss. It develops coordination and balance, and prevents injuries resulting from weak muscles and joints.

How much muscle is desirable is very much an individual decision. The degree of muscularity considered physically attractive varies greatly from person to person and between sexes. Men usually desire more muscular 'bulk' whereas women may be more concerned with 'toning' muscles.

Although illegal and potentially very harmful, many professional bodybuilders take performance-enhancing drugs such as anabolic steroids in an attempt to build more muscle. These simply upset the body's natural internal hormonal environment, and can be harmful in the long run. The risks associated with taking these drugs are many and varied, and include testicular atrophy and subsequent sterility in men. In women there can be development of male characteristics, acne, liver damage and mood swings.

Weight Training

Weight training, also known as strength training, affects different individuals to a different degree. It is not possible for all persons, engaging in the same exercises, to elicit a similar response. Every individual has genetic characteristics that will affect the way they change their body shape in response to weight training.

Weight training carries with it all the benefits of anaerobic exercises. It can be safely prescribed to all young, healthy adults. There may be a problem when middle-aged and elderly persons do weight training as there can be a sudden rise in the blood pressure due to unaccustomed effort. There can also be a sudden strain on the heart, as well as the bones and joints.

Weight training is safe when properly supervised and controlled. Every weight room should have a set of rules and regulations pertaining to safety and they should be on public display. Rules may vary from one gym to another but some very basic rules apply to all individuals engaging in weight training

What are the benefits of weight training?

- The most effective way to change the body's physical appearance.
- The only means of increasing the size and density of muscles. Weight training helps directly in losing body fat and gaining muscle.
- Increases stamina, strength and endurance.
- Causes deposition of calcium in bones and prevents osteoporosis.
- Involves neuromuscular adaptations as well as morphological adaptations in response to physical stress. Neuromuscular adaptations involve motor development, contraction efficiency, and efficient transmission of nerve impulses. All these result in improved coordination.
- Increases flexibility and speed.
- Sports enthusiasts, including runners and cyclists who believe in being lean and sinewy rather than bulky, have consistently shown an improved performance after four to six weeks of weight training.
- Improves your metabolism. You burn calories all through the day.
- Strengthens the back muscles and other joints of the body, and help in preventing arthritis at all ages.
- Increases the utilization of glucose in the body. This decreases the possibility of developing adult-onset diabetes mellitus.

Weight training has three components, *intensity* (weight), *frequency* (how often) and *duration* (how long). These three have an inverse relationship with each other. If one component is decreased, increasing one or both the others can compensate. For example, if you exercise less often, that is decrease the frequency, you can increase the duration and the intensity.

How do you get started?

Educate yourself. The more you know, the sooner you will realize your goals, and the lesser will be your chances of tissue trauma. Learn everything about training before you start. Learn the right technique. Find a teacher, if possible.

Start slow. Start with 500-gram weights if you are a beginner. Do not try too much too soon. Start with one set per muscle group. Increase reps before you increase weights. When you can easily do twelve reps, increase weights by 500 grams.

Find the right weights. Do not choose too light a weight. The last two reps should require a little effort, i.e. they should not seem too easy. Work with muscles through their full range of motion. Lift at a speed that you can control, so that you can stop if you want to. Train first at high volume and low intensity—with more reps and less weight. Later, increase the intensity and decrease reps. If you cannot finish a set, decrease the number of reps. If you find you are grunting or pulling faces, you are probably lifting too much weight. On an average, each rep should last 4 seconds: 2 for lifting and 2 for bringing it back.

A *rep* is one movement carried out in its entirety, or one execution of an exercise. For example, moving a dumbbell through 90° and back is a rep. A *set* is the same movement repeated anything between (ideally) eight to twelve times or more, with little or no pause in between. So a certain number of reps constitute a set.

Remember your goals. For fitness, use light weights and many reps. For body building you need to use higher weights.

Beginners should always start with light weights, irrespective of their goals.

Exercise in order. Exercise large muscles, such as back, thighs and chest first, as these fatigue more quickly. Later you can go on to smaller muscles such as biceps and triceps. If you have to do both aerobics as well as weight training, start with weight training. If you start with aerobics, you will feel too tired to lift weights and you will not be working at optimum intensity. You will also compromise on technique, and increase your chances of injury.

For hormonal stimulation and weight loss, do the aerobics first. This will deplete blood glucose and stimulate fat metabolism for energy.

For optimal muscle gains you can do the anaerobic before the aerobic. This will allow for plenty of blood glucose energy for the weight lifting anaerobic portion of your programme.

Start simple. Start with single joint movements, such as biceps curls. Multiple joint movements, such as squats, where you squat down while raising a weight at the same time, should be left for bodybuilders.

Control your breathing. While lifting weights, remember to breathe easily. It is a good idea to exhale during peak effort. Breathe out while applying power (lifting). Breathe in while bringing a weight back, or between reps.

Be consistent. Train all the year round. People get deconditioned and much more susceptible to injury if they have erratic training periods.

Listen to your body. Do not stick to a programme stubbornly if it does not seem suitable for you. Your programme should feel right, it should not leave you too exhausted so that you can hardly crawl out of bed on the following day. Some people need more rest than others, as their tissues require time to adjust to the rigours of training.

Eat correctly. If you go on a crash diet, you will not only lose stamina, you can actually lose muscle mass. Take a balanced diet with plenty of complex carbohydrates and proteins. After a workout, the body cells are most receptive to replenishing the lost energy, so take a meal within an hour of your workout.

Do not be a 'workoutaholic'. Do not train feverishly as if there is no tomorrow. Do not assume that more is better.

Do not get discouraged. It takes time to see a change in the body. Be prepared for this.

Volume is the total number of sets and reps performed at each training session. Low-volume training means doing very few sets—maybe only one. You can do low-volume training at high intensity, that is using very heavy weights. High-volume training is where small weights are used and many sets are performed.

How does overload affect muscle mass?

Better performances can be the product of a number of factors, such as efficient technique, the progression of endurance, all round strength and general mobility. Weight training is the most widely used and popular method of increasing strength. For a muscle to gain size, it must be taxed to a maximum, which usually means that you should be doing at least eight to ten reps or one set. Increasing the number of sets increases endurance. To increase strength, simply increasing the number of sets is not enough; you have to increase the weights as you go along.

A muscle will only strengthen when forced to operate beyond its customary intensity. This intensity is known as overload. When overload increases, there is a subsequent enhancement of performance, power and even muscle size in later stages.

Overload can be progressively increased by increasing one of the following:

- Resistance: adding extra weights
- Number of reps with a particular weight
- Number of sets of the exercise
- Intensity: reducing the recovery periods

What is muscle fibre hypertrophy?

Resistance training will ultimately increase the muscle size. This is known as muscular hypertrophy. Muscle growth is due to one or more of the following adaptations:

- Increased contractile proteins (actin and myosin)
- Increased number and size of myofibrils per muscle fibre
- Increased amounts of connective, tendinous and ligamentous tissues
- Increased enzymes and stored nutrients

Which weight training exercises should be performed?

The exercises must be specific to the type of strength required. Exercises should be identified that will produce the desired development. However, every good schedule should also include some of the following:

- Bench press
- Squats
- Sit-ups
- Shoulder press
- Lateral raises
- Lower back raises
- Triceps curls
- Crunches
- Bicep curls
- Hamstring curls
- Shoulder shrugs
- Lunges

These general exercises give a balanced development, and provide a strong base upon which highly specific development can be undertaken.

What is meant by 1RM and RM?

Find out what is the maximum amount of weight you can lift in one go. This is referred to as one repetition maximum (1RM), the weight at which you can do only one rep.

The maximum number of reps in a particular set that you can perform before fatigue sets in, is referred to as repetition maximum (RM). This reflects the intensity of the exercise.

How much weight you should be using for weight training depends on your 1RM. Calculate 60–80 per cent of 1RM. You should ideally be training using this load, and you should work towards attaining this goal over a period of days and weeks. It is better to start with less weights and more reps, and gradually increase weights till you reach your target and then continue training with this.

Note: Do not start exercising at 1RM.

How many sets and reps should you do?

One set of 8–12 RM performed three days a week is a typical strength training programme. The greatest strength gains usually result from working with 4–6 RM. Working with 12–20 RM facilitates the increase in muscle endurance and mass.

The optimal number of sets of an exercise to develop muscle strength remains a matter of debate. A number of studies comparing multiple-set programmes and single-set ones indicate that there is no significant difference.

Using heavy weights for weight training will require a recovery of 3–5 minutes between sets. The amount of time you should spend on recovery is again, like your exercise menu, an individual feature. If enhancing endurance is the aim, only minimum recovery should be taken.

How often should you do weight training?

Three times a week is the ideal. The body must be allowed to recover from the strenuous demands of weight training. It is better to embark on the next session only when the muscles are more or less entirely free from soreness or fatigue. As a rule of thumb 48 hours should elapse between sessions.

Some trainers recommend that you should vary the workout to such an extent that the weights used are different each time. This is especially true for athletes, or those training for an event. Those who work with very heavy weights will find it extremely difficult to maintain the same level of lifting at each session, and the total poundage lifted in each session would be better to be varied (e.g. a high-, low- and medium-volume session) each week.

What sort of weight-lifting equipment should be used?

There are variable resistance machines and free weights. Most trainers prefer free weights.

Free weights (barbells, dumbbells and machines that provide the same equal resistance to a muscle) allow you not only to target a particular muscle group but to engage other muscles that assist in the work. Barbells and dumbbells are easy to use and convenient, and one can start with a small weight and increase gradually, as recommended. The assisting muscles help stabilize the body, support limbs and maintain posture during a lift. Lifting free weights improves coordination by improving the neuromuscular pathways that connect muscles to the central nervous system. The mind has to be focussed on the particular movement, and muscles and nerves have to essentially follow orders given.

Variable resistance machines are effective tools for building strength and muscle tone and are designed to work the target muscle in isolation, without the assistance of the surrounding muscles

Training Systems

Simple Sets: These should be followed by all those who are starting weight training. You should do a small number of sets, each with say 8 reps, with 20 per cent of 1RM. (e.g. 3 x 8 with 20 per cent—meaning 3 sets of 8 reps with a weight of 20 per cent of maximum for 1 repetition.) This is the system that all novice lifters should work on, because the high number of reps enables the lifter to learn correct technique, and thereby reduce the risk of injury.

Pyramid System: This is not for beginners. Here the load is increased and the rep are reduced (e.g. 100 kg x 10, 120 kg x 5, 130

kg x 4, 140 kg x 3, 150 kg x 2, 160 kg x 1). Pyramid lifting is only for experienced lifters who have an established good technique.

Super Setting: This consists of performing two or three exercises continuously, without rest in between sets, until all exercises have been performed. The normal 'between sets' rest is taken before the next circuit of exercises is commenced.

How can you re-stimulate progress?

In the beginning, novice weight trainers seem to make progress no matter what they do. Later, it becomes increasingly difficult to make even the smallest gains. Even the most productive exercises lose their effectiveness over time. One way of attempting to re-stimulate progress is to change the exercise routinely executed for a particular muscle group. Any significant change in your routine can stimulate new progress.

Change in exercise simply spurs the body to added effort. When a new exercise has been introduced, the progress for the first few weeks is largely due to neural-motor adaptations. After this initial 'learning or relearning' phase, subsequent strength increases are predominately morphological; muscles get slightly larger.

But do not overdo the change. Changing exercises for a muscle group at every workout is not necessary, and may even be harmful, for you are, for all intents and purposes, utilizing your options too fast. Consequently, you may be left with very few options in re-stimulating progress for future workouts. In addition, it becomes difficult to make progress if you change your exercises too frequently. Your muscles, tendons, ligaments, joints, vascular elements and neural-motor units respond favourably to small increases in the duration and intensity of exercise. It is very difficult to use the ideal resistance if you change your exercises every workout.

Systematic increases of reps and resistance can easily be achieved by performing the same exercises for at least a few weeks.

For beginners, the best exercises are those you are comfortable in performing. For more advanced trainees, the most effective exercises are those they are not as familiar with. For continued relative strength gains, continue the same exercise in your weight-training routine for four to eight weeks. After which, restructure your workout with a different basic exercise for each muscle group.

What is meant by pump and burn?

Immediately following a weight-training exercise the muscle may seem full and tight for 15–30 minutes. This is what is commonly called a pump. It is caused by trapped plasma within the muscle. During muscular contraction the muscle diameter increases as it shortens. During intense contraction there is an inward force which occludes the blood vessels momentarily. Blood surges into the muscles and pools within it. A compensatory increase of blood pressure forces plasma from the congested capillaries into the interstitial spaces of the muscle cells. This causes the pump.

Bodybuilders commonly perform pumping exercises before appearing on stage. For most people there is no real benefit from achieving a pump. Inability to achieve a pump is one symptom of over-training. This happens because over-training leads to the depletion of the glycogen reserves in the muscles. As a result, fluid volume in the muscle, and possibly blood volume, decrease.

The burn is simply a feeling of soreness in the muscles. This burning sensation during certain weight-training exercises or high-repetition training is caused by an accumulation of lactic acid in the fatiguing muscle. Anaerobic glycolysis utilizes carbohydrates and produces water and lactic acid, or free hydrogen ions. This acid does not clear sufficiently if blood flow is impeded. Whenever a muscle contracts intensely for a prolonged period of time, the blood vessels within that muscle get occluded. The outflow of toxins from the muscle is therefore blocked, lactic acid accumulates, which acts upon nerve receptors to produce the localized burning sensation.

Should you do high-volume or low-volume exercises?

Bodybuilders and athletes traditionally did high-volume, low-intensity workouts (several sets using light weights). The disadvantage of this is that you may not put full effort into the initial stages of the workout as you are aware that you have many sets to do. With repeated effort, fatigue would set in, and it would become progressively difficult to train with maximum effort. Also, you end up spending a lot of time, and overuse injuries are common.

The latest recommendation for power lifters, suggested by the American College of Sports Medicine, is that one should do one warm-up set followed by one workout set at high intensity.

It is important that intensity is maintained. If intensity is steadily decreased over a period of time, muscle mass will deteriorate. In order to prevent decrease of intensity, it is important to ensure that duration should not be unduly prolonged.

To maximize the muscle mass, low-volume, high-intensity exercises have been found to be the best. Ideally, you should decrease the time spent in weight training, and utilize it for aerobic activities where duration is much more important.

If you are a beginner, you should start with high-volume exercises using light weights, keeping in mind that you have to progress to low-volume, high-intensity exercises, in order to maximize the muscle mass.

Low volume exercises result in greater strength gain. Recovery between workouts is faster. There are fewer injuries due to overuse. Also, they can be done quickly.

If you are in the advanced category, again low-volume exercises are best for you.

The Right Setting

Unless you are playing a sport or exercising out of doors, you need to pick an environment you are comfortable in to work out. Your choices are usually two: either in a gym or health club, or at home. The choice depends on what is convenient for you.

Is joining a gym or health club worthwhile?

A good gym or health club can provide tremendous fitness opportunities by way of equipment, training, supervision and, what is more important, the motivation to keep going. Gyms are especially useful for those who exercise better if there are other people around with similar objectives.

Before you choose a gym or health club, you should visit several and look around closely. You should also decide your exercise programme before you go, so that you can check that it has all the facilities that you require. If your goal is aerobic fitness, see that there are adequate cardiovascular machines such as treadmills, power steppers, exercycles and rowing machines. If you are interested in weight training, check the equipment and its condition. If the place is offering an aerobics class, check that there is a wooden floor.

Checklist for choosing a gym

- ☐ Is the gym large, well lit and airy?
- ☐ Does it have all the equipment you want to use?

- ☐ Is all the equipment in good working order?
- ☐ Are the instructors trained and competent?
- ☐ Do they make you undergo a fitness test before you start?
- ☐ Do they enquire about your medical history?
- ☐ What is the staff-client ratio?
- ☐ Do the instructors spend time with each client?
- ☐ Is the attitude of the staff attentive, courteous and encouraging?
- ☐ Are the surroundings clean and hygienic?
- ☐ Do the other clients look happy?
- ☐ Is there a doctor who gives a check-up to all new clients?
- ☐ Is there life-saving equipment in working order and oxygen?
- ☐ Is the atmosphere conducive to working out?
- ☐ Is there a first aid expert, who can carry out cardiopulmonary resuscitation?
- ☐ Do they have single-sex hours (if you are uncomfortable exercising with those of the opposite sex)?

Checklist for choosing a swimming pool

- ☐ Is the pool at least 25 metres long?
- ☐ Does the water look and smell clean?
- ☐ How often is the water changed?
- ☐ Is there a trained instructor?
- ☐ Are there lifeguards posted down the length of the pool?
- ☐ Are the changing rooms clean and do the showers work?
- ☐ Does the pool insist on a shower before you swim?
- ☐ Are the regulars wearing swimming caps?
- ☐ Are the surroundings clean and hygienic?
- ☐ Do the other clients look happy?
- ☐ Is the atmosphere conducive to working out?
- ☐ Do they have single-sex hours (if you are uncomfortable exercising with those of the opposite sex)?

Apart from the actual facilities, there are other things that need to be considered which are equally crucial.

Supplementary checklist

- ☐ Is it close to your house or workplace so that you can go easily?
- ☐ How expensive is it?
- ☐ Is there adequate parking?
- ☐ Is it accessible by public transport?
- ☐ Are there water fountains and locker facilities?
- ☐ Is there a support group?

Some gyms or health clubs offer discounts for couples and senior citizens, or have seasonal offers, or group discounts. Some allow you to pay for the use of the gym or pool by the hour, which can be handy if you are using them as a supplementary activity.

Is setting up a home gym worthwhile?

You may have experienced the desire to work out in the comfort of your home, so that you save on commuting, get to spend more time with the family, or watch a favourite TV programme which is on at the only time when you have time to exercise. Inclement weather or sheer laziness may make the prospect of going to the gym unenticing.

If there is no good gym nearby, and if you are certain that you are going to use it regularly, it may be worth setting up a home gym.

If you are starting up an exercise programme and plan to work out at home only, you can structure your routine so that the facilities at home are adequate. Many of the exercises described in the following section can easily be done at home, if you invest in a pair of dumbbells.

Do you really need a home gym?

- **Will you use the equipment regularly? How committed are you to working out? If you invest in expensive equipment like a treadmill or an exercycle, are you sure it will not end up as a clotheshorse?**

- **Can you afford it? You can work out at home with just a pair of dumbbells and regular furniture, so you should consider carefully before you invest in more expensive equipment.**
- **Will the equipment help you meet your goals? Do not believe tall claims: abdominal exercise machines that make flab disappear from your waistline or treadmills that melt away an amazing number of calories in an hour. It is not the machine that burns calories, it is you. Unless you are prepared to make the effort, no machine can help you reach your goal.**
- **Do you have room for it? Do not buy equipment unless you have space to keep it. Having to store the equipment, or worse, having to disassemble it, will be a deterrent. Space being a constraint in large cities, it is better to buy one machine that fits in easily in the bedroom, rather than purchasing several large pieces of equipment, which might never come out of their packing crates. Buy strictly what you need and what you will use, not more.**

The markets are flooded with equipment of all kinds, and manufacturers make many claims for their efficacy. However, before you choose, you should be aware of what precisely you are looking for.

How do you select equipment?

- What type should you buy? You need to define your goals before you select equipment. Do you need to work out the lower body only? Buy a treadmill or an exercycle. If you are looking for a full body workout, try a rowing machine or an exercycle with upper-arm levers. Do you want to go for muscle definition? Buy dumbbells. Do you wish to combine both aerobic and anaerobic activities? Walk on a treadmill and add a few dumbbell exercises. You should try every kind of machine in a gym before you select what you want for your house.
- Is the equipment made according to specifications? It is generally better to buy from reputed brands, who are less likely to come up with a defective piece of equipment, than local brands. Check the machine thoroughly. Compare with the catalogue and see if

all is in order. Go through individual features one by one, such as adjustment levers and electronic devices. Check for stability. Sometimes it is hard to tell from just looking. It is a good idea to wear your workout gear to the shop and try out the machine. It should feel solid and durable.

- Is the equipment comfortable? Some people believe that the more discomfort they are giving their bodies, the stronger they will emerge. However, if exercising is not comfortable, you will be tempted to discontinue. All exercise equipment should be easy to use. A machine can be well made but still feel awkward. You should always test the equipment exhaustively in the shop. Pay attention to how your lower back, joints and muscles feel. The seat should stay comfortable during a long exercise session. Bars or handles should be padded and feel easy on the hands, even after many minutes. Note the noise level and ease of using the controls. Is the machine making a sound that grates on your nerves? Do pedals or tracks creak or squeak after every rotation?
- How much money should you spend? If you are setting up a home gym with anything more than a pair of dumbbells, you should be prepared to spend at least a few thousand rupees, more if you are buying several pieces of equipment. If you buy the more sophisticated machines which measure heart rate, calories burnt, time elapsed or have built-in calculators, you will have to pay more. These are useful features, but not absolutely necessary for most people. Programmable machines that can automatically adjust the workload may not be worth the price, since manual controls, if accessible, work just as well.

Average Prices

Treadmills	Rs	25,000–1,00,000
Rowing machines	Rs	5,000–17,000
Exercycles	Rs	3,000–30,000
Steppers	Rs	4,000–45,000

What is a treadmill?

A treadmill is a moving strip on which you are compelled to keep on walking or jogging, otherwise you will fall off. Treadmills have the advantage that you can do your exercise indoors, you need not go out, thus you are independent of weather conditions. You can switch on some music at the same time. Music sets not only the mood but the pace itself, and you tend to walk along with the beat.

You can walk, jog or run on a treadmill. Walking is the simplest. It stresses the joints least, but jogging and running will burn more calories per minute.

What features should you check?

- Surface: This can be soft or hard, but it should be shock absorbent. If you are planning to run or jog, investing in a surface with more 'give' is worth it. Even for walking, it is better to have a surface that is soft.
- Inclined track: This is of immense use to those who are serious about exercising. Walking briskly up an incline increases the resistance against which you are working, and can provide the same intensity as jogging. A 1.25–1.5 horsepower motor will be required in order to move the treadmill track upward.
- Length: The treadmill belt should still be at least 5 feet long. If you are running, you need a bigger and wider belt.
- Handrails: There should ideally be handrails on either side, which can support your weight should you lose your balance.
- Exterior: It should have a sturdy metallic frame.
- Digital display: You can have computerized treadmills which display time, speed, distance, pulse rate and calories consumed.
- Alarm: This is beneficial for the elderly and cardiac patients. The alarm goes off if your pulse rate rises and an electronic switch automatically switches the machine off.

- Instant pull-off switch: This is emergency cord which stops the treadmill. It is beneficial for the elderly and for heart patients.

How should you use the treadmill?

- You should get familiar with the equipment before you start.
- Always start at a low speed.
- Walk normally. Initially, you can hold on to the handrails in order to maintain your balance. But this invariably reduces the workout intensity.
- Once you have mastered the technique, keep your hands off the rails whenever possible.
- When walking or running on a slant, maintaining good posture with only a slight bend at the waist is best for your back.

What is a stationary bike?

Exercycles or stationary bikes are perhaps the most popular home gym equipment. They provide fairly intense workouts with little investment. They take up little room; some can be folded. They can be pushed into a living room, in front of a TV set, and in an instant the couch potato turns into a fitness fiend.

What features should you check?

- Mechanical or electronic brakes: Bikes that have electronic brakes adjust pedal resistance automatically to keep the workload constant as pedalling speed changes. In bikes with mechanical brakes you can adjust the resistance of your workout by simply adjusting a knob. The work rate increases as pedalling speed increases. Thus, you can make the workout harder by either adjusting a resistance knob or pedalling faster.
- Rubber grips: Avoid bikes that add resistance with rubber grips or pincers that grip the wheel. These may look very attractive in a store, but they give a jerky ride, which usually lacks the feel of riding a bicycle altogether.

- Recumbent (reclining) design: These bikes have a comfortable seat with a back rest that reduces strain on the lower back and spine. The low position ensures good circulation in the leg muscles.
- Arm cranking: Some models have arm cranks, and the arms can be moved backward and forward, again by adjusting a lever. You can change the resistance of the workout. Arm-plus-leg exercise burns more calories than cycling alone, and provides variation in the workout.
- Digital display: If you can afford it, an exercycle which shows pulse rate, time, speed, distance and calories consumed is ideal.
- Adjustable height.
- Transport rollers.

How should you use the bike?

- You should get familiar with your equipment before you start.
- Position handlebars comfortably.
- Set the seat height according to your own height. When seated, your knee should be bent only slightly with the pedal at its lowest point.
- Adjust resistance
- Use pedal clips to fix your feet firmly in place on the pedals. This will allow your legs to pull as well as push the pedals.

What is a rowing machine?

Rowing provides an excellent cardiovascular workout. Although rowing seems to work mostly the upper body, a proper rowing stroke gets 70 per cent of its force from the trunk and legs.

What features should you check?

- Electrical or mechanical machines: Electrical machines are superior as they are more adjustable and you have access to important information (speed, pulse, calories consumed).

- Hydraulic or wind resistance: Mechanical machines are of two kinds: hydraulic or wind resistance. The latter offers a more natural feel, as do electric rowers.
- Seat: A smooth-running roller seat that moves back and forth freely is recommended.
- Resistance: Choose a machine that offers uniform resistance throughout the rowing motion.
- Digital display: If you can afford it, buy a machine which shows pulse rate, time, speed, distance and calories consumed.
- Non-slip footplates: These should have safety straps and be height-adjustable.
- Transport rollers.

How should you use the rowing machine?

- You should get familiar with your equipment before you start.
- If you have rowed before, you will find a rowing machine easy to use. Otherwise, you need to practice before you can get the stroke right.
- Sit upright to avoid back strain.
- Do not overarch your back as you complete each stroke.
- Keep your elbows close to your body when pulling.
- Breathe naturally. Do not hold your breath while pulling.

What is a power stepper?

It provides an excellent form of aerobic exercise, especially good for your buttocks, thighs and legs. However, if you suffer from vertigo, you should avoid steppers. People with a tendency to motion sickness also find steppers hard to use. It takes up very little space.

What are the benefits?

This again gives a good aerobic workout. As little as 10 minutes of stair climbing is sufficient to give an intense workout, and that too without exposing your legs to severe impact forces.

What features should you check?

- Adjustability of settings: For height and stepping speed.
- Comfortable handrails.
- Built-in twister: Some machines have this option for exercising the upper body.
- Digital display. If you can afford it, the machine should show pulse rate, stepping speed, height achieved, time and calories consumed.

How should you use the power stepper?

- You should get familiar with your equipment before you start.
- Stepping height ranges from about 2–8 inches. Keep the pedals in the mid-range without touching the floor.
- Stand upright. Keep your knees vertically over your feet. Do not stoop or lean forward.
- Keep your feet flat on the pedals to reduce stress on your Achilles tendon.
- Hold the handrails lightly for balance.

The Right Gear

If you are going to start an exercise programme seriously, it is worthwhile to invest in the right gear. This need not be expensive, as long as you know your requirements and examine your options carefully. However, you need to be conscious of quality.

The type of clothes and shoes you need depend on your exercise programme, where you are planning to work out, and the place where you live.

- Quality is important. It is better to have one good quality outfit suited to your needs than several cheaper ones.
- As expenditure on clothes and shoes is not something which will recur frequently—provided you buy good quality products—it is worthwhile making the initial investment.
- Although the right clothes and shoes may not enhance performance, they help to avoid discomfort or even injury.
- Both outerwear as well as innerwear have to be selected according to your requirements.

How do you choose the right shoes?

You may feel overwhelmed by the choice that you are faced with when you go to buy shoes. There are many brands, colours and types.

- You should match your shoes to your exercise programme: the kind of exercise and the frequency. If you do not focus on only one activity such as walking, jogging or racquet sports, all-purpose cross-training shoes are the best option. But if you do a certain sport or activity three or more times a week, shoes specific to that sport or activity will help you avoid injuries.

Different kinds of shoes

Aerobic shoes **must hold your feet firmly and should have shock absorbency under the ball of the foot. They should have a lot of impact-absorbing cushioning to prevent foot injuries.**

Cross trainers **are ideal if your exercise schedule encompasses a wide spectrum of activities. These shoes are designed for stability. They are not suitable for frequent running or high-impact exercises. If you are doing more than an occasional aerobic class, cross trainers are not suitable.**

Running shoes **are primarily made to absorb shock as the heel strikes the ground. Look for light, durable uppers in quick-drying fabric. The heel should be higher than the front of the shoe in order to prevent calf muscle and Achilles tendon strain, and there should be cushioning to absorb impact. Running shoes give no protection against side-to-side movement, so are not suitable for racquet sports.**

Tennis shoes **provide more stability. For tennis and for all other court sports, you need shoes that help keep the ankle stable during side-to-side movements, which means that the sole should not be too thick. Tennis shoes come with lateral stabilizing straps and stiff heel support. They should be well fitting, but with a slim cushioning at the base, so that the ankle does not get twisted inadvertently.**

Walking shoes **allow the foot to roll and push off naturally during walking. They usually have a fairly rigid arch, a well-cushioned sole, and a stiff heel support for stability. The heel should be higher than the rest of the shoe. Some degree of shock absorbency is necessary. They should be stable from side to side, and well-cushioned with extra shock absorption at the heel. Most of the time, jogging or running shoes fit the bill very well when it comes to walking.**

- You need to know your feet and their requirements, especially the shape. Every shoe manufacturer uses a different basic shoe shape. Some companies make shoes that are shorter or longer than those made by other companies, even if they are of the same size. Some fit a wide foot perfectly, while others are cut for a slimmer foot.

Does the shape of the foot matter?

Yes, it does. You should know whether your foot is narrow or wide at the toes, so that you may buy shoes accordingly. The same sports shoe company may have shoes of different width in the same shoe size.

You should also know if your feet have high, medium or low arches. It's easy to tell which kind you have. Just wet the bottom of your bare foot and make a footprint on a hard surface. Or you can smear your sole with a thin solution of ink and water, and place it on paper lightly, as you would during walking. Do not press too hard. Now check the imprint. If the forefoot and heel areas are connected by a thin line, you have high-arched feet. If the footprint looks pretty much like the shape of your foot, you have a low arch. A medium arch falls somewhere in between. High-arched feet are not very flexible—you should buy cushioned shoes. If you're flat-footed, your feet are too flexible, and you need motion control shoes. Those who have medium arches would request something in the middle, sometimes called a stability shoe.

- Your previous foot problems should be kept in mind before you make a purchase. For example, if you have a history of ankle sprains, you need shoes which give maximum ankle support. If you have bunions, choose a shoe with a wide 'toe box'. If you are flat-footed, you may need arch support. If you have corns, callosities, bunions or other problems, consult your chiropodist about the best shoe for you. Some people require extra padding to be put inside their shoes, while some require wide or open-toed shoes to prevent pressure on corns.
- You should go to a shop which specializes in sports shoes where the assistants can help you in your choice.
- It is often useful is to visit the shoe shop late in the afternoon, when your feet are slightly swollen. This approximates the condition

they will be in after you have been working out for some time. Wear the same kind of socks to the shop as you do when working out. If you use orthotic devices for your feet, make sure you wear them when you're trying on your shoes.

- Choose shoes for their fit, not by the size you've worn in the past. It is quite likely that shoes that fitted you well five years ago may not be so comfortable today. With age, your foot size will change. The length of the foot may stay unaltered, but the width does increase, and the foot tends to get wide and flat as age advances. It's important to have both the length and width of your feet measured every time you shop for shoes. Be sure to have the salesperson check the fit of both shoes for you when you are standing up. If you bend over to check it yourself, you will change the position of your foot in the shoe.
- The widest part of your foot should be in the widest part of the shoe. The sides of your foot should not extend over the sole of the shoe. This means that the base or sole of the shoe should be as wide as the sole of your foot. Your foot should not move from side to side inside the shoe.
- Try on at least four or five pairs of shoes. Put on and lace both shoes of each pair and walk around for a minute or two, before you decide. Try some of the movements you would do while exercising.
- The material should be flexible and allow your feet to breathe.
- Shoes should not be too heavy but at the same time should not be too light and flimsy.
- You may generally like the feel of a softer shoe, but it might not last as long as a firmer one. Very thin or flimsy shoes like canvas sneakers can worsen some problems such as calf or Achilles tendon pain.
- A shoe whose heel compresses too easily is harmful in the long run, though it might feel very comfortable initially, for extra heel compression can overstretch your calf.

- Check shoes for flexibility. Soles that bend at the ball of the foot, not under the arch, offer better support.
- It is very important that the shoes should fit well. The heel should be snug. You should be able to move your toes in the shoe, and there should be one-half to a full thumb's width between the end of the longest toe on your longer foot and the end of the shoe.
- After you've found a pair that you think fits well, walk or run a little in the shop—some stores even have a treadmill for that purpose. The shoes should feel comfortably snug—neither tight nor too loose—and you should not feel the stitching or seams on the inside of the shoes.
- Before buying, check the quality with the vertical heel test. Place the shoe on the shelf and make sure the heel is straight up when looked at from the back. Check other points as well. Is the midsole well connected to the upper? Is the stitching complete? Check inside the shoe for any irregularity, hardness, unevenness, rough patches or bumps.

How should you take care of your shoes?

New sports shoes should feel comfortable immediately. If they do not, you have not made the right purchase. However, new shoes are not meant for immediate heavy-duty use. You need to allow some time for the shoe to adapt to your foot, and your foot to feel at home in the shoe. Do not play an important match or run a marathon wearing new shoes. This period of conditioning can take anything from a week to a month, and only after that can you get maximum mileage from your shoes.

Keep checking your shoes for signs of wear and tear. Monitor their condition as they age. The first sign of ageing may be a feeling of diminished comfort. If you are into competitive sports, your performance may deteriorate a little. After you have done 300–500 miles, the cushioning on most shoes wears out. If you do a sport or activity regularly and for long periods, it may be worth investing in two or three pairs of shoes and rotating them.

Checking for ageing

Place your old shoes on a table or other flat surface and look at them carefully. Are the edges badly worn? Have you worn out holes in the soles or uppers? Do your shoes stand straight or are they leaning backward or forward or slopping sideways? If this is so, it's probably time for a new pair.

Even if your shoes appear to be in good shape, you should buy a new pair if you've logged 500 or more miles in them. Worn-out shoes may be a factor if you have started getting pain in your feet, ankles, legs or knees though you haven't changed your exercise routine.

Another way to check for ageing is to try on a new pair of that same model. You may not realize how much your shoes have worn until you compare them with a new pair.

Because the insoles in most shoes are made for immediate comfort, not extended use, they often break down quickly. When your original insoles wear through, you can replace them with off-the-shelf insoles.

Keep shoes in a cupboard away from dust and grime. If you have been walking in damp weather, let your shoes dry thoroughly, then flake off mud deposits. Now wash thoroughly and dry again. Let shoes air dry between uses. You can even alternate pairs to ensure thorough drying.

Buying children's shoes

Children's shoes may need to be replaced every six months, depending on the child's rate of growth. But as children may walk and run hundreds of miles in each pair of shoes, it is worthwhile investing in good quality running shoes rather than thin-soled canvas ones. Children need good cushioning, support and protection in their footwear, and shoes should not squeeze their growing feet. While you can allow for some growing room, the heel should not slip up and down, and the forefoot should not move side to side in the shoe.

If you buy shoes with Velcro closures, get the best quality shoes available so that stability is not compromised. Even with shoes which the child will not use for specifically sporting purposes, remember that children invariably run around a lot, so never buy shoes with rigid soles.

How should you care for your feet when working out?

It is not enough to buy good shoes, a general foot care regime should be maintained if you are working out regularly, especially if you are walking or running.

- Wear thick, absorbent socks.
- Dry feet well after bathing,
- Use powder before putting on shoes.
- Nails should be cut regularly, straight across the toe.
- Self-treatment of corns and calluses with over-the-counter remedies before starting to walk can do more harm than good.
- If blisters develop, visit your doctor. Self-treatment by opening the blister with a sterilized needle and draining the fluid is acceptable, but only in emergencies. Do not remove the 'roof' of the blister. Cover the treated blister with antibiotic ointment to guard against infection.
- If itching develops, remember to keep your feet very dry. Dry between the toes. Sprinkle anti-fungal skin powder liberally before wearing your shoes.

How do you choose the right sports innerwear?

All people who exercise should opt for appropriate sports undergarments. Wearing the right innerwear can minimize discomfort due to chafing and skin rashes.

Sports bras: Women need sports bras to avoid the discomfort of bouncing breasts, especially if they are large-breasted. Sports bras provide the necessary control. There are many technologically designed, superior ones available in the market which are not only comfortable and functional, but stylish and fashionable as well.

What to look for in a sports bra

- **Fabric: Cotton minimizes stretch and gives a good support. A combination of cotton with a fabric resembling lycra mesh that absorbs sweat is a good option.**
- **Seams: The seams should be such that they do not chafe the skin.**
- **Stretch: There should be little or no vertical stretch in the fabric. Some horizontal stretch is permissible to allow for breathing.**
- **Fit: The fit should be comfortable but not tight.**
- **Shoulder straps: Wide cotton or elastic straps that do not slip are the best.**
- **Movement: The entire upper body should move as one, once the bra is comfortably in place, with no bouncing.**
- **Mobility: Many sports bras are shaped like halter tops. Check that the armholes allow ample room for the unrestricted arm movements necessary during exercise and for freedom from chafing.**

Sports briefs: Men need sports briefs in order to prevent injuries. They provide support and some protection by keeping the genitals close to the body, keep sweat from building up and minimize chafing.

Different kinds of sports briefs

- **The jockstrap is used by those who participate in contact sports to prevent direct injury.**
- **Cotton briefs provide good support, unless they are soaked with sweat. They are not meant for those who are into high-impact exercises**
- **Compression shorts are by far the best bet. They provide support, elasticity, firmness and are usually made of a breathable fibre that does not allow sweat to accumulate.**

How do you choose the right sports outerwear?

This is paradoxically the most flexible area as far as sportswear is concerned. You should wear what you are most comfortable in, keeping in mind the climate and the activity you are participating in. Your clothes should be comfortable and loose, and the fabric should breathe. They should be suitable for your activity. It is not necessary to buy the latest fashions in sportswear, but it makes sense to buy good quality clothes that can withstand the frequent washing that your workout gear requires.

Indoor workouts: Shorts and a vest or T-shirt are a good choice for almost all indoor work, or you can wear a light track suit if required. Lightweight socks in a breathable fabric are a must. Some women like to wear a leotard with leggings or a unitard for indoor aerobic activity.

Outdoor workouts: A warm tracksuit is useful when it is cold. You can wear a cotton T-shirt under it. You may need to invest in a wind- and waterproof jacket if the climate demands it, as well as gloves. A scarf or hooded jacket top can protect the head and back of the neck from cold injuries. Too many layers are better than too few for outdoor wear. It better to wear several thin sweaters than one heavy one—as your workout progresses and you feel warmer, you can discard one layer at a time. Do not carry discarded clothing in your hands while walking or running as they can throw your body out of gear. It is better to wrap a jacket or pullover around your waist.

In warm weather, a light tracksuit, or shorts and vest provide the maximum comfort and give the most freedom. Lightweight drawstring trousers in cotton that provide easy mobility can be a good option.

How do you choose the right swimming costume?

Swimming costumes are designed to minimize 'drag' in water. Chlorine tends to fade the colour of swimwear. It may even lead to early rot of fibres.

It is best to buy a well-fitting costume that reduces drag and washes well. Shoulder straps should be secure, and not sagging.

Nose and earplugs are a good idea, and goggles a must. A swimming cap protects the hair from the bleaching action of chlorine and cuts down on drag. Some people use webbed gloves to utilize the resistance of water, but this is optional.

The 20-Minute Action Plan

The Programmes

This section outlines easy-to-follow 20-minute programmes which can be carried out within the confines of the home, and which even the most busy person will be able to follow. With as little as 20 minutes a day, you can indeed become fitter than what you are, and if you are conscientious and regular, you will gain in strength, endurance, flexibility and overall fitness.

You need to plan your workout under three broad categories:

1. Flexibility
2. Strength
3. Aerobic fitness or stamina

A word of caution

At the beginners' level, it would be best to practice exercises involving weights (dumbbells or barbells) using a light stick instead of the actual weight in order to learn the precise steps and movements of the exercise. Only when you have mastered the technique should you proceed with actual weights.

The programmes outlined are of two kinds: one for beginners, and one for those who having been exercising regularly. Subsequent chapters describe the exercises in detail.

Step 1: Judging your level

Before you begin you should make a preliminary judgement of your fitness level, based on the parameters given below, in order to select your programme. The two categories—beginners and advanced—are not hard and fast, and many people would fall somewhere in an intermediate category. Therefore it is important for you to work out which programme is better for you. It is always better to start from the beginners' programme and work your way up.

A word of caution

Remember that it is important to warm up and stretch before you start on any workout, and to have a cooling off period at the end of each workout.

Beginners

You are a beginner if one or more of the following hold true for you:

1. **You never exercise.**
2. **You are more than 45 years of age.**
3. **You have a known medical problem.**
4. **Your resting heart rate and your recovery pulse rate are in the poor or fair category (*see pp. 25–27*).**

Advanced

You are in the advanced category if all of the following are true for you:

1. **You exercise regularly, more than three to times per week.**
2. **Your are less than 45 years old.**
3. **You have no current or past medical problem.**
4. **Your resting heart rate and recovery pulse are in the good or excellent category (*see pp. 25–27*).**

A word of caution

If you are in the advanced programme but you cannot cope with it, go back to a beginners' menu. Starting with a beginners' programme does not mean that you will take longer to get to the desired level of fitness. It is better to start slow and then build up, rather than injuring yourself or finding the challenge so great that you give up altogether.

Step 2: Choosing a menu

Choose a menu that is appropriate to your fitness level.

Step 3: Maintaining a scorecard

Maintain a daily scorecard. This will chart your progress, help in continual assessment, and will accommodate your day-to-day notes. A scorecard should read something like this:

A word of caution

If you are above 50, take things slowly. Work at half the rate prescribed, and build up gradually. If you are above 60, find the pace that suits you best, beginning at an appropriate level. Slow the pace if required. At all times, keep your goal within sight.

DAY 1/WEEK1: Flexibility				
	Exercise	*Reps*	*Total time*	*Notes*
1	Arm swings	6	30 seconds	Managed comfortably
2	Back and up reach	6	30 seconds	
3	Shoulder roll	8	45 seconds	
4				

DAY 1/WEEK 1: Strength					
	Exercise	*Sets and Reps*	*Weight*	*Total time*	*Notes*
1	Dumbbell curls	2 x 8	500 gm	1 minute	Could have done another set
2	Triceps dips	2 x 8	500 gm	1 minute	Very tiring
3	Shoulder press	2 x 8	500 gm	1 minute	Should move to 1 kg
4					

DAY 1/WEEK 1: Aerobics				
	Exercise	*Distance*	*Total time*	*Notes*
1	Outdoor walking		5 minutes	Could have walked faster
2	Treadmill walking		3 minutes	Good workout
3				
4				

The specific details of exercises are outlined in the following two chapters.

BEGINNERS' MENU: Weeks 1 to 4				
Time	*Category*	*Frequency*	*Exercises*	*Notes*
5 minutes	Warm up	Daily	Arm swings Side arm reach Shoulder roll	
	Flexibility	Daily	Neck stretch Overhead stretch Triceps stretch Chest raises Knee hug Standing groin stretch Quadriceps stretch Upper calf stretch Total body stretch	Hold each stretch for 6–8 seconds Do each exercise 4–5 times
5 minutes	Strength	Monday, Wednesday, Friday, Sunday	Lunges Squats Wall press-ups	Spend about 90 seconds on each exercise
		Tuesday, Thursday, Saturday	Lower back raise Calf raises Dumbbell curls	Spend about 90 seconds on each exercise
5 minutes	Aerobics			At fast pace
3 minutes	Cooling	Daily	Aerobics	At slower pace
2 minutes			Stretches	Sustain each stretch for 20 seconds

BEGINNERS' MENU: Weeks 5 to 10				
Time	*Category*	*Frequency*	*Exercises*	*Notes*
5 minutes	Warm up	Daily	Arm swings Side arm reach Shoulder roll	
	Flexibility	Daily	Neck stretch Overhead stretch Triceps stretch Chest raises Knee hug Standing groin stretch Quadriceps stretch Upper calf stretch Total body stretch	Hold each stretch for 6–8 seconds Do each exercise 4–5 times
10 minutes	Strength	Monday, Wednesday, Friday, Sunday	Triceps curls Shoulder press Crunches Flat bench press Lateral raise Lower back raises Bottom raise Hamstring curls	Spend about 90 seconds on each exercise
	Aerobics	Tuesday, Thursday, Saturday		
3 minutes	Cooling	Daily	Aerobics	At slower pace
2 minutes			Stretches	Sustain each stretch for 20 seconds

Note: In weeks 5 to 10, you are doing a full 10 minutes of either weight training or aerobic exercises. After ten weeks, increase the time for this section of the programme by adding a minute a day to a maximum of 20 minutes. The warming up and cooling off periods will be in addition to this.

ADVANCED MENU: Weeks 1 to 4				
Time	*Category*	*Frequency*	*Exercises*	*Notes*
4 minutes	Warm up	Daily	Arm swings Side arm reach Shoulder roll	
	Flexibility	Daily	Neck stretch Overhead stretch Triceps stretch Chest raises Knee hug Standing groin stretch Quadriceps stretch Upper calf stretch Total body stretch	Hold each stretch for 6 to 8 seconds. Do each exercise 4 to 5 times
1 minute			Jumping jacks	
10 minutes	Strength	Monday, Wednesday, Friday, Sunday	Triceps curls Shoulder press Crunches Flat bench press Lateral raise Lower back raises Bottom raise Hamstring curls Advanced lunges Advanced squats Upright rows Forward raise Shoulder shrugs Double crunches Bicycling	
	Aerobics	Tuesday, Thursday, Saturday		At fast pace
5 minutes	Cooling	Daily	Aerobics	At slower pace
			Stretches	

ADVANCED MENU: Weeks 5 to 10

While the warm up and cooling parts of the routine remains the same, the time spent on aerobics and strength training should be gradually increased to 20 minutes.

Do not do all the strength exercises on each day of the week. Split your exercises in two groups as follows:

Monday, Wednesday, Friday, Sunday: exercises for back, chest and shoulders.

Tuesday, Thursday and Saturday: exercises for abdomen, upper and lower limbs.

ADVANCED MENU: Week 11 onwards

Continue with 10 minutes of aerobics and 10 minutes of strength training regularly. Add variety to your routine to prevent boredom.

Split Routine

This means working the same body parts on alternate days. For example, you work the arms, legs and abdomen on odd-numbered days, and back, shoulders and chest on even-numbered days. This is a good way to prevent fatigue as the muscles get full 48 hours to recover from strength training. Unless the exercises are very mild, as in the beginners' routine, it is important not to work the same body part on consecutive days.

How should you structure your workout?

1. Do not force yourself to stick to the menu given above. Be flexible in your workout routine. If after two weeks you find the beginners' menu too simple, try the one meant for weeks 5–10.
2. If at any point of time, you feel that the work is difficult, take a small step backward. For example, if the weights seem excessive, cut down on weights by 500 grams. If this is more comfortable then continue with these for two weeks before moving on to a larger weight. If the aerobic exercises you are doing leave you gasping, decrease the pace and intensity, but try and sustain it as far as possible.
3. Remember to work out the larger muscle groups before the

smaller. This maintains efficiency, and also ensures that the smaller muscle groups get adequate blood supply.

4. Add variety to your workout by following a split routine.
5. Use different weights for different muscle groups depending on what you are comfortable with. You might be able to do dumbbell curls with 2-kilogram weights, but you might find it impossible to do lateral raises with the same weight. Do not push yourself too far, do not force a very heavy weight on your muscles. Remember, strength training should be a pleasure, not a punishment.

Warm Up and Stretching Exercises

Why warm up?

Unless your body is properly warmed up, your muscles and tendons are less pliable, and will be less able to cope with the demands of exercise. If you exercise without warming up adequately, you increase the risk of injury.

Warming up is not merely about limbs. A good warm up should increase the heart rate gradually so that it can pump blood around the body to meet the increased demands of the work out.

Basic position: This is the position at which most exercises begin. This will be mentioned in many of the exercises that follow.

Stand with your eyes facing forward, feet shoulder-width apart, toes turned a little outward, as shown in the diagram.

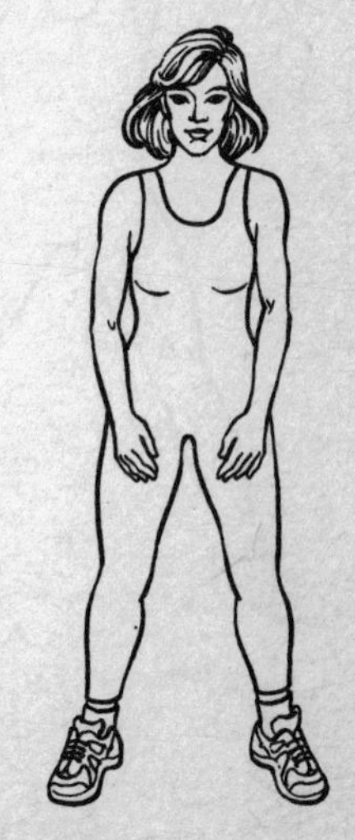

You can also warm up by doing the aerobic activity you plan to do at a very gentle level. For example, if you are going to run, you can begin by walking for a few minutes, and then gradually increase the pace until it becomes a fast walk or a jog.

Arm Swings

- Begin from the basic position.
- Cross hands in front of the hips.
- Take a deep breath in.
- Swing your arms outward, and take them over your head.
- Breathe out as you swing your arms back to starting position

Side Arm Reach

- Begin from the basic position.
- Place left hand on the hip, and the right one over your head.
- Bend from the waist and lean to the left.
- Return to the basic position.
- Repeat with your right hand on the hip and left overhead.

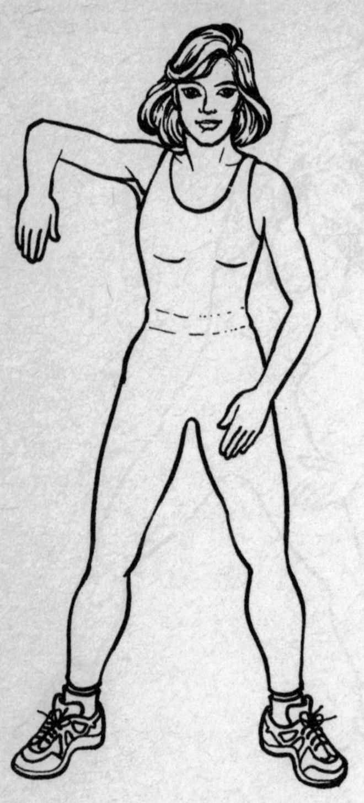

Shoulder Roll

- Begin from the basic position.
- Roll your right shoulder forward and up, then bring it back and down.
- Repeat in the reverse direction, i.e. bring your right shoulder back and down, then forward and up.
- Repeat with the left shoulder.

Back and Up Reach

- Begin from the basic position.
- Slowly extend your left arm straight up.
- At the same time extend your right arm down and back, as far back as is comfortably possible. Hold briefly.
- Repeat, changing arms.

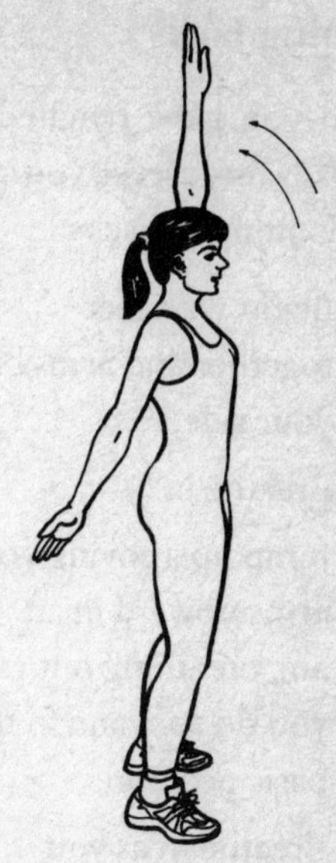

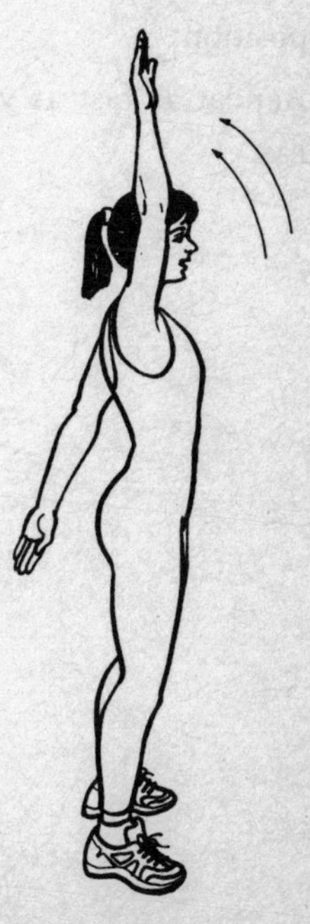

Jumping Jacks

When you have reached a more advanced level, you can also do jumping jacks.

- Begin with feet together and arms by your side.
- Breathe in.
- Jump up, moving your arms upward in an arc, breathing out as you do so. Land in the basic position.
- Breathe in as you jump back to starting position.
- Repeat as fast as you can.

Why stretch?

Stretching scores over all forms of exercise when your goal is flexibility.

As age advances, the range of movement of the various joints of the body tends to decrease. This starts when you are in your twenties, but may go unnoticed for several decades as it proceeds slowly. Often you notice it only in late middle age.

It is important to keep the tissues around the joints pliable to ensure the full range of movement. This also slows down the onset of degenerative disorders such as arthritis or osteoporosis.

Fitness and flexibility are not the same thing. Sports persons can be very fit when it comes to a particular group of muscles, but they may lack flexibility in the remaining body areas. For example, a cyclist may have strong and well-developed calf muscles, but his shoulder joints may not be in that good a shape. It is important to try to achieve all-round flexibility, even if you participate in a specific sport.

When you stretch, you should try to continue the stretch until you can feel a slight tension in the muscles. Hold the stretch at that point, for at least 6 seconds. You should try to hold each stretch for longer as you progress.

It is important to enjoy the stretches. While stretching, imagine the blood flowing into your limbs. Thinking peaceful thoughts prevents tension of muscles and joints and thus promotes stretching.

Developmental stretches

When you hold a stretch for twenty to 20–25 seconds this causes the muscle fibres to lengthen and is known as a developmental stretch.

A word of caution

Do not stretch when you are feeling cold. Make sure that you are warm enough; wear an extra garment if required.
Avoid doing stretches first thing in the morning.
Developmental stretches are best done when the joints are loose and flexible as in the afternoons or evenings.

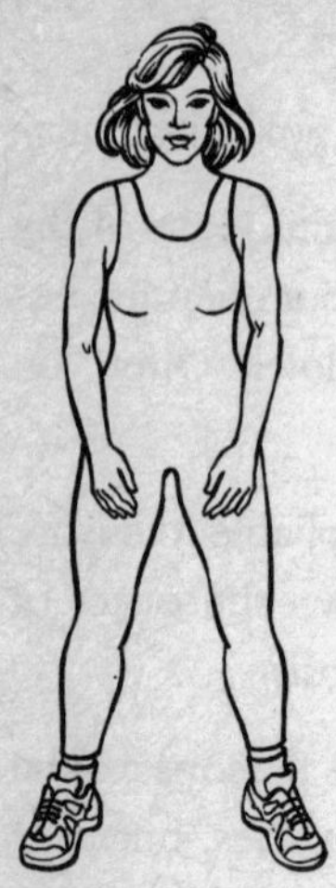

Neck Stretch

Muscles worked: Neck.

- Begin in the basic position. You can also do this exercise sitting down.
- Slowly tilt your left ear towards your left shoulder as far as it will go. Do not lift the shoulder.
- Hold the stretch.
- Return to starting position.
- Repeat on your right side.

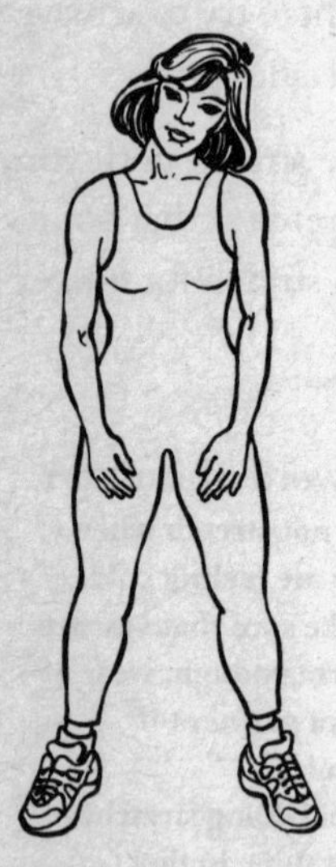

A word of caution

Never throw your head right back to stretch the back of your neck. This can damage the spine.

Overhead Stretch

Muscles worked: Deltoids, back and obliques.

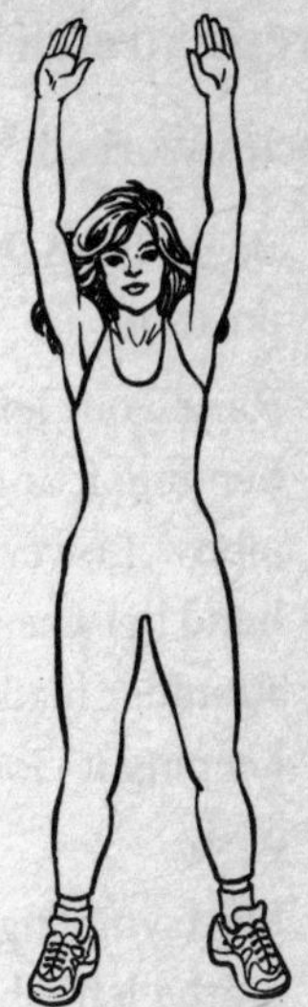

- Begin from the basic position.
- Raise your arms as far up as possible, keeping the palms facing forward.
- Cross your wrist and place your palms together.
- Keep your head up and look forward.
- Hold the stretch.
- Repeat, with the wrists crossed in the opposite direction.

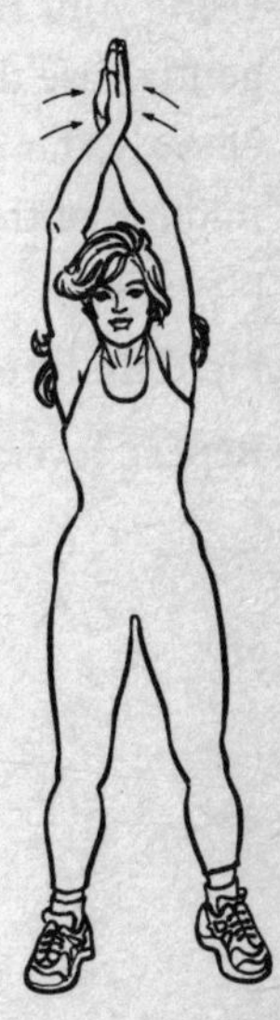

A word of caution
If you are a beginner do not attempt to cross the wrists. Simply press your palms together.

Triceps Stretch

Muscles worked: Triceps.

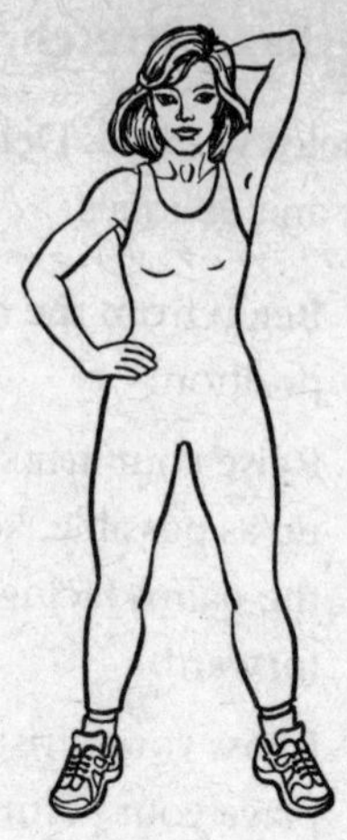

- Begin from the basic position.
- Raise your left arm, bending it at the elbow. Lower your hand between your shoulder blades, keeping it close to the body.
- Place your right hand on the left elbow.
- Using your right hand, gently ease the left elbow as far down the midline of the body possible.
- Hold the stretch.
- Repeat, reversing hands.

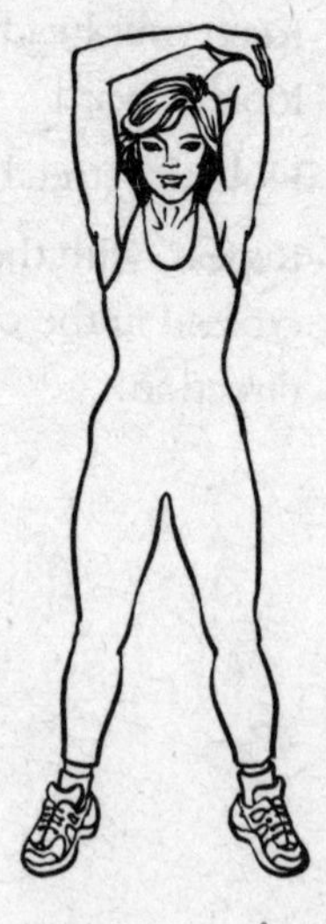

Chest Raise

Muscles worked: Pectorals.

- Lie face down, with your hands interlocked and resting on your buttocks.
- Slowly raise your arms till you feel tension in your chest.
- Hold the stretch.

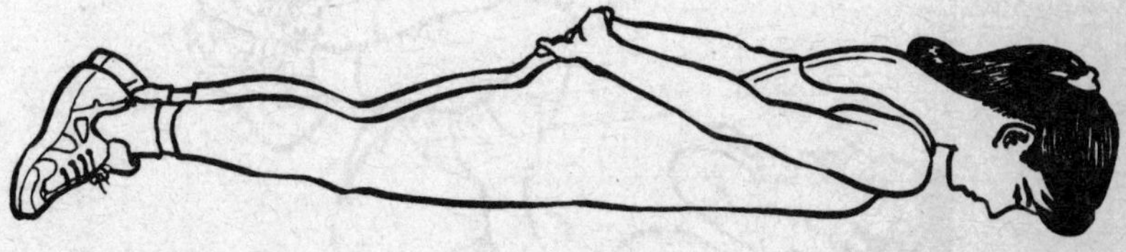

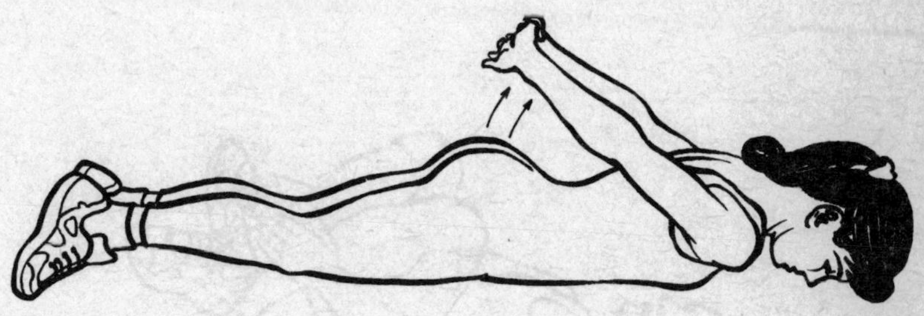

Knee Hug

Muscles worked: Gluteals.

- Lie on your back.
- Placing your hands behind your knees, lift your knees upwards.
- Cross your feet at the ankles and move your hands down to hold the ankles.
- Slowly draw your knees towards your chest.
- Hold the stretch.

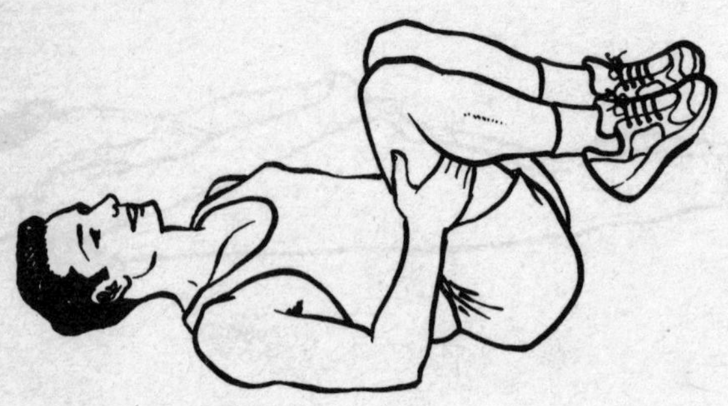

Standing Groin Stretch

Muscles worked: Quadriceps and inner thighs.

- Begin from the basic position.
- Keeping your left leg straight, take a big step to the right with your right leg.
- Bend your right knee and turn your right toes outwards by 45°.
- Press your weight gently to the right, onto your right heel.
- Hold the stretch when you feel a mild tension in your groin.
- Repeat, changing legs.

Quadriceps Stretch

Muscles worked:
Quadriceps.

- Begin from the basic position.
- Rest your hands gently on the back of a chair or against the wall.
- Raise your right leg. Hold the right ankle in your right hand.
- Gently ease your foot towards the buttock.
- Hold the stretch when you feel a mild tension in the front of your thigh.

A word of caution
Do not arch your back during the stretch or jerk your foot while moving it upwards.

Calf Stretch

Muscles worked: Back of lower leg.

- Begin from the basic position.
- Rest your hands on the back of a chair.
- Take a big step backward with your right leg.
- Bend your left knee.
- Transfer your body weight forward, keeping your back straight.
- Hold the stretch.

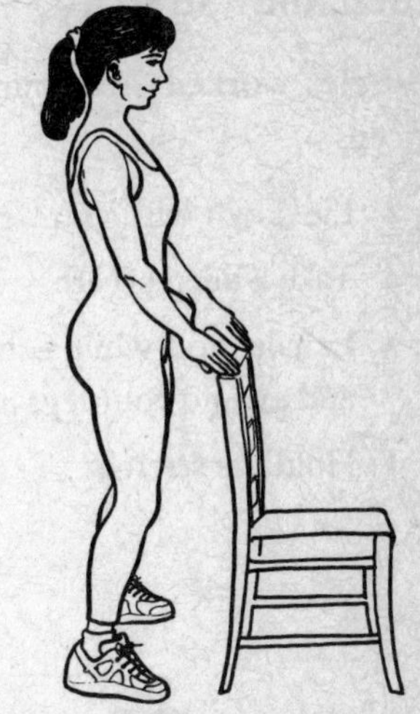

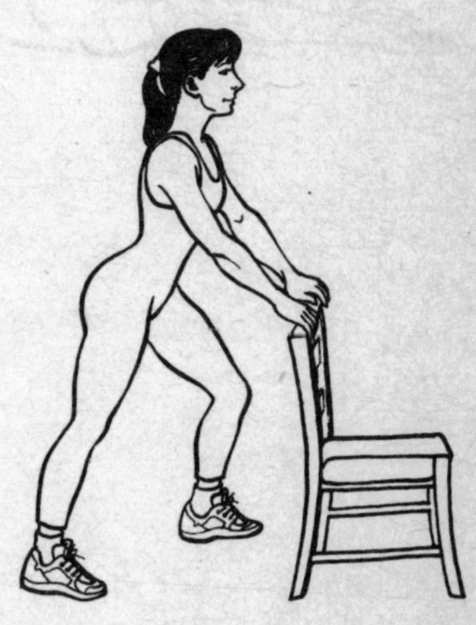

A word of caution

Do not tilt your back forward or bend to the side during this exercise. Keep your feet on the ground, do not stand on your toes.

Total Body Stretch

Muscles worked: Abdominals, obliques, trapezius, quadriceps and triceps.

- Lie down with your feet together, arms by your side.
- Take a deep breath.
- Exhale, and while exhaling, extend both your arms overhead and extend your legs as far as possible.
- Hold the stretch.

Exercises for Strength

A word of caution
Do not be in a hurry. Start with light weights. Increase the weight only when you are able to do five or more sets with great ease. Do each exercise slowly. Unless stated otherwise, exhale when you exert maximum force.

In order to increase strength, some of the exercises need to be done with weights. Any exercise that involves the use of weights should be done with caution and, more importantly, with the right technique. Both faulty technique and the use of wrong weights can cause injuries.

What is the right weight?

The right weight is one that makes the last couple of reps a challenge. If you are doing eight reps, for example, you should be able to do the last two, but it should take quite a bit of effort. If you are feeling sore at the beginning of the set, discard the weight for a lesser one.

If you can complete the set without any sense of effort, increase the weight by 500 grams and restart.

What is the right way to hold a weight?

It is vital to grip the weights correctly. This ensures the technique is correct, prevents injuries, and makes exercising easier.

To hold dumbbells or barbells, use an overhand grip. Your thumb should come

A word of caution
Check the instructions carefully before starting the exercise. It is a good idea to have a dummy drill before you actually pick up the weights.

under the weight with your knuckles up. Keep your wrist straight and locked. Do not bend your wrist unless stated.

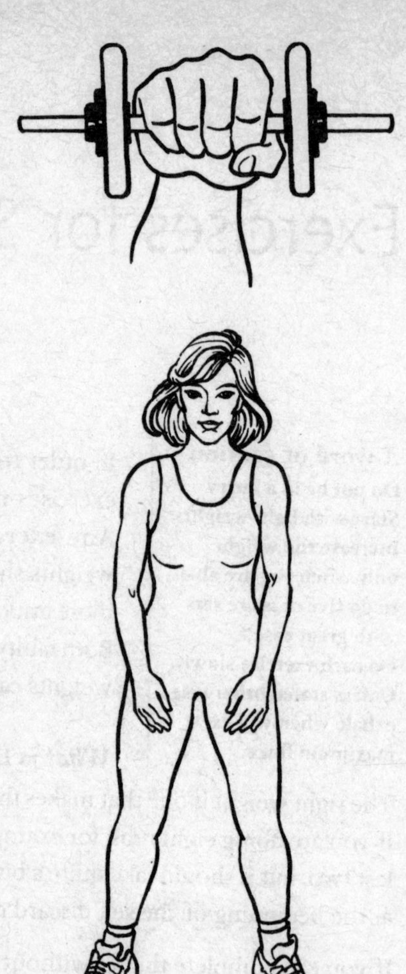

What is the correct posture?

Stand with your feet hip width apart, with toes pointing forward. Keep your spine straight, shoulders back and stomach in. Look straight ahead, not down. This is known as the primary position.

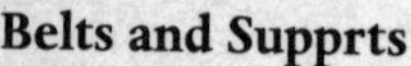

Belts and Supprts

Many people wear a belt or wrap when doing weight-bearing exercises. They contract the muscles around the spine, abdomen and rib cage, thereby increasing pressure within the abdomen and stabilizing the spine. They are especially useful if you are doing weight lifting or squats using heavy weights.

Lunges

Muscles worked:
Quadriceps, hamstrings and gluteals.

Recommended level:
Beginners (Weeks 1 to 4).

- Begin from the primary position.
- Breathe in as you take a step forward with your right foot.
- Bend your left knee and lower it towards the floor, as far as is comfortably possible.
- Breathe out as you draw your right foot back and stand upright.
- Each set should have eight to ten reps.
- Repeat with the other foot.

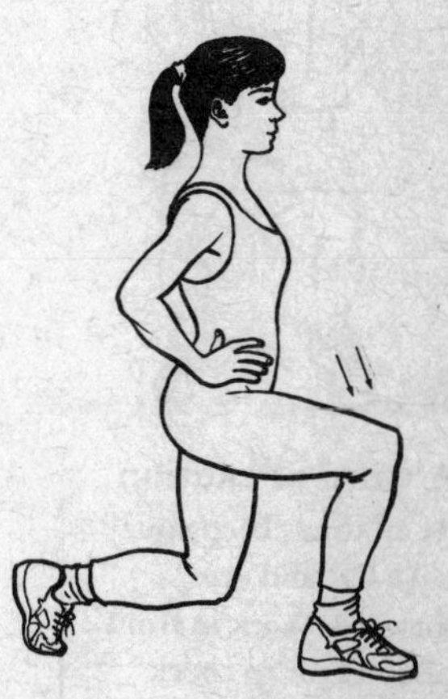

A word of caution

Beginners should not lower the leg at the back right up to the floor. You should stop about 6–8 inches from the floor. As you make progress, aim to get a little closer.

Squats

Muscles worked:
Quadriceps, hamstrings and gluteals.

Recommended level:
Beginners (Weeks 1 to 4).

- Begin from the primary position. Rest your hands on your hips.
- Breathe in as you bend your knees and slowly squat down. Your posture should be as if you are sitting on an imaginary chair. Do not let the squat go beyond seat height.
- Breathe out as you stand up.

A word of caution

At all times keep your back flat and eyes forward. Work in front of a mirror to check that your body is aligned correctly. Do not allow your back to arch. Do not squat too far down. Taking a squat too far, i.e. below seat level, puts the muscles and tendons at the knee joint to severe stress, and can be dangerous.

Calf Raise

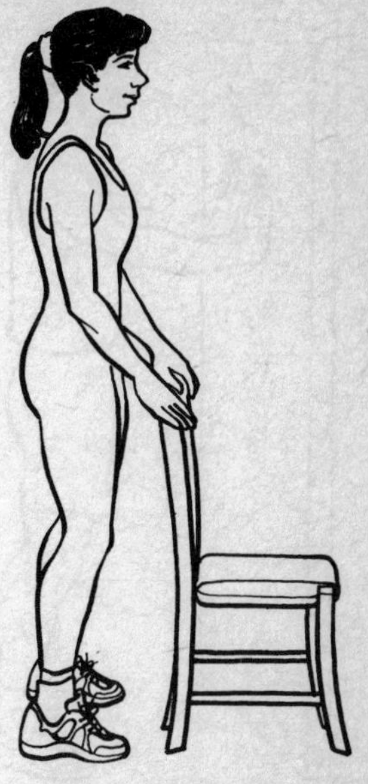

Muscles worked:
Gastrocnemius.

Recommended level:
Beginners (Weeks 1 to 4).

- Begin from the primary position.
- Look forward. Rest your hands on the back of a chair.
- Breathe out as you lift your heels off the floor, so that your weight is on the balls of your feet and toes.
- Hold briefly.
- Breathe in as you slowly lower your heels back to the floor.

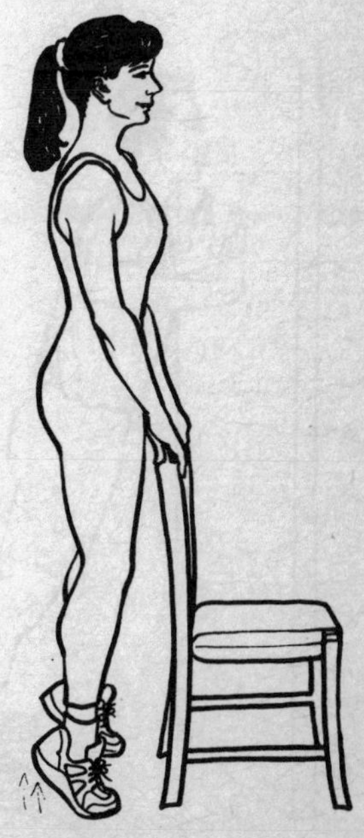

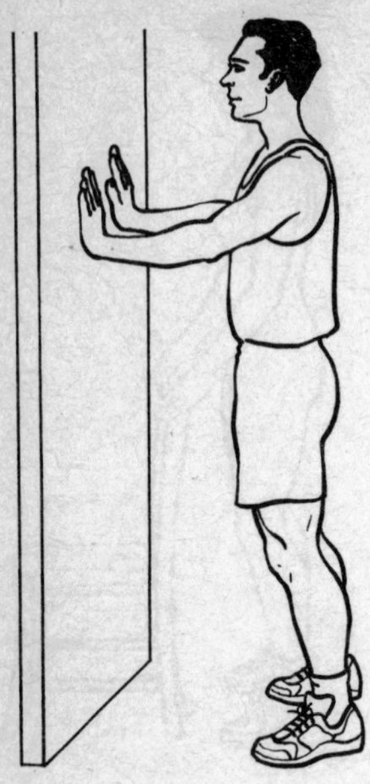

Wall Press Up

Muscles worked: Deltoids, pectorals and triceps.

Recommended level: Beginners (Weeks 1 to 4).

- Begin from the primary position, with your feet 2 feet away from a wall.
- Place your hands flat on the wall, in line with your shoulders, and palms facing upwards. Look forward.
- Breathe in as you bend your elbows and lean towards the wall. Keep your back straight. Aim to touch the wall with your nose.
- Hold firmly, then straighten your elbows.

Back Raise

Muscles worked: Lower and middle back.

Recommended level: Beginners (Weeks 1 to 4).

- Lie face down, feet together.
- Stretch your arms forward, keeping them on the floor.
- Breathe out as you raise your right arm and the left leg at the same time. Avoid jerky movements.
- Hold briefly. Repeat with the left arm and right leg.

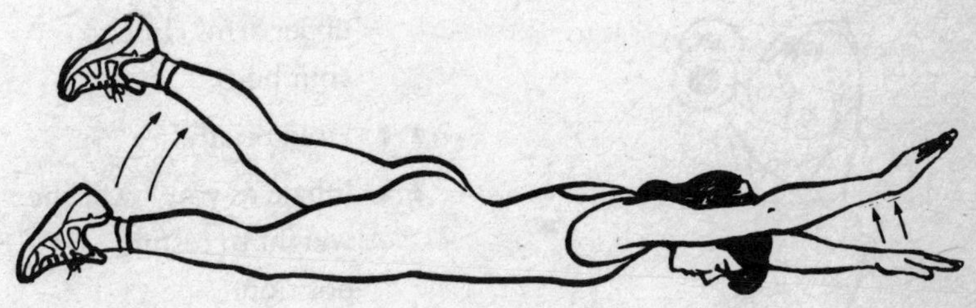

Dumbbell Curls

Muscles worked: Biceps and brachialis.

Recommended level: Beginners (Weeks 1 to 4).

- Begin from the primary position.
- Take an underhand grip on a pair of dumbells, and hold them close to the thighs, palms facing forward.
- Breathe out as you slowly raise the dumbbells towards the shoulders, flexing the elbows. Keep your upper arms close to your body.
- Hold briefly.
- Inhale as you lower the weight to resting position.

Note: Avoid swinging the dumbbells. There should be no movement at the shoulder joint or the wrist. Only the elbow should move.

Triceps Curls

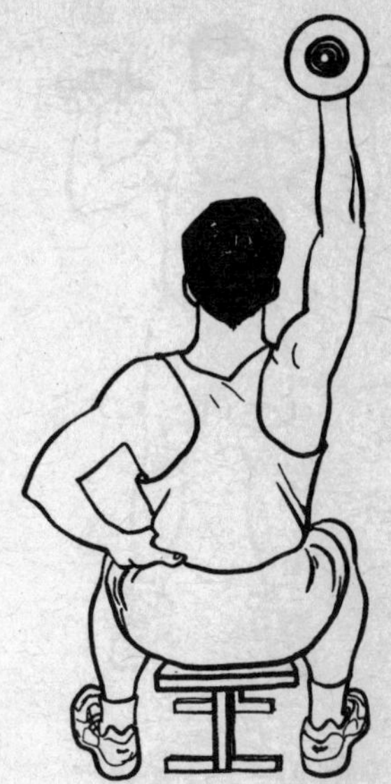

Muscles worked: Triceps.

Recommended level: Beginners (Weeks 1 to 4).

- Begin from the primary position. Alternately, you can sit on a chair with your feet flat on the floor.
- Hold a dumbbell in your right hand, palms facing inward. Lift the dumbbell straight up.
- Inhale as you lower the dumbbell beneath your shoulder blades, behind your neck.
- Exhale as you lift the dumbbell back.
- Repeat to complete a set.
- Repeat with the other hand.

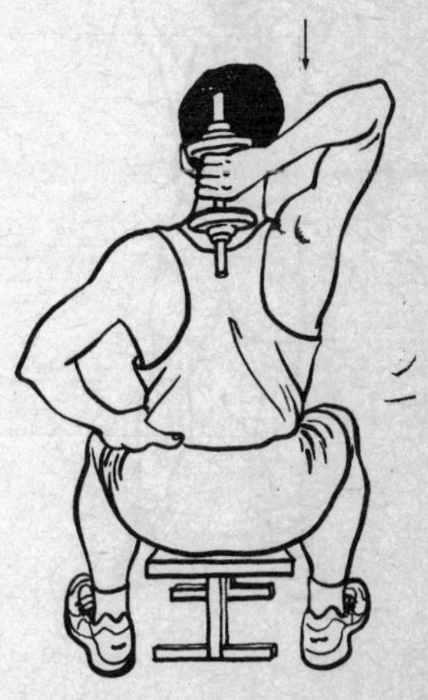

Shoulder Press

Muscles worked: Deltoids, trapezius and triceps.

Recommended level: Beginners (Weeks 5 to 10).

- Begin from the primary position.
- Lift a pair of dumbbells and hold them at the level of the shoulders, with palms facing forward.
- Exhale as you raise your arms upward towards the ceiling.
- Inhale as you lower arms to resting position.
- Repeat to complete a set.

A word of caution

Keep your back straight and eyes facing forward. If you lean back, you risk straining your back.

Crunches

Muscles worked: Abdominals.

Recommended level: Beginners (Weeks 5 to 10).

- Lie flat on your back with your knees bent and hip-width apart. Keep your feet flat on the floor.
- Place your palms on the front of your thighs.
- Breathe out as you raise your shoulders off the floor. Slide your palms towards your knees as you rise upward.
- Hold for a few seconds, then breathe in as you slowly lower your shoulders to the floor.
- Repeat to complete a set.

A word of caution

A small movement is enough. Do not attempt to sit right up.

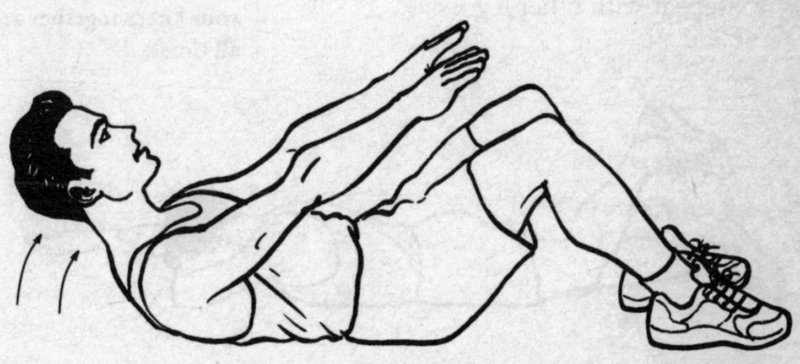

Hamstring Curls

Muscles worked: Hamstrings and gluteals.

Recommended level: Beginners (Weeks 5 to 10).

- Lie face down on the floor.
- Rest your head on your left forearm and stretch your right arm out in front of you.
- Raise your left leg off the floor, so that your knee is about 2 inches off the floor.
- Breathe out as you curl your left foot towards your buttocks.
- Hold briefly.
- Breathe in as you slowly lower your leg to 2 inches off the floor.
- Repeat to complete a set.
- Repeat with other leg.

A word of caution
Remember to keep the working knee off the floor. This will ensure that you are working your hamstrings. Keep your knees together at all times.

Bottom Raise

Muscles worked: Gluteals.

Recommended level: Beginners (Weeks 5 to 10).

- Lie face down on the floor.
- Rest your head on your left forearm. Extend your right arm in front of you, palms facing downwards.
- Breathe out as you raise your left foot as high as possible.
- Hold for a few seconds.
- Lower your leg.
- Repeat to constitute a set.
- Repeat with other leg.

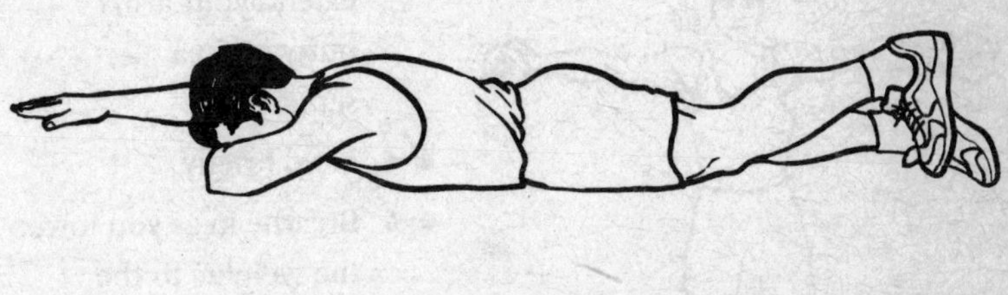

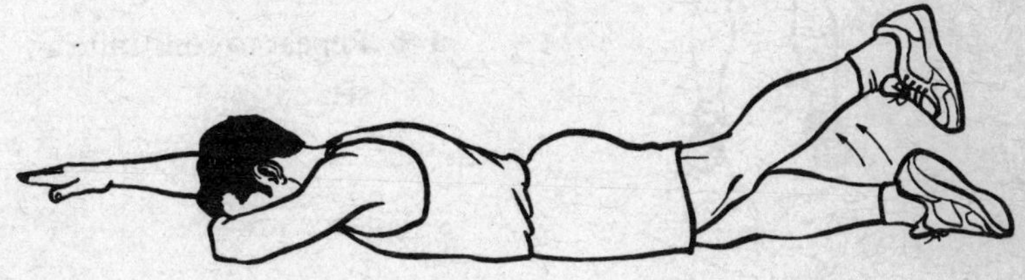

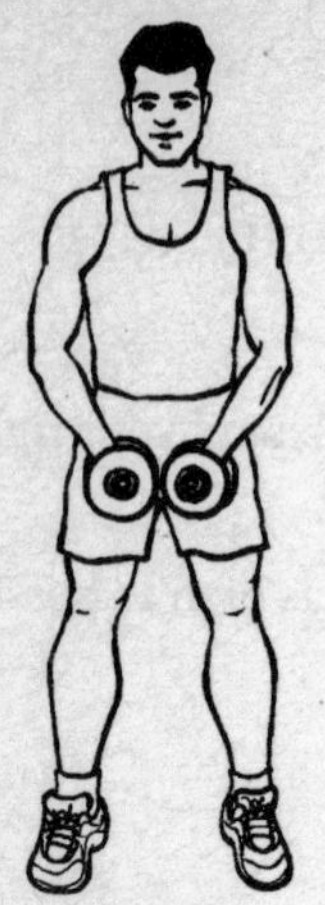

Lateral Raise

Muscles worked: Deltoids.

Recommended level:
Beginners (Weeks 5 to 10).

- Begin from the primary position.
- Lift a pair of dumbbells to the front of the thigh, palms facing inwards.
- Bend your elbows about 30–40°.
- Breathe out as you extend your arms outward in a semicircle.
- Hold briefly.
- Breathe in as you lower the weights to the front of the thighs.
- Repeat to constitute a set.

A word of caution
Do not lock the elbows when you are raising your arms. Do not raise your arms beyond shoulder height.

Lower Back Raise

Muscles worked: Lower back.

Recommended level: Beginners (Weeks 5 to 10).

- Lie face down, with feet together and toes pointing to the floor.
- Place your hands on your buttocks.
- Breathe out as you raise your upper body off the floor.
- Hold briefly.
- Lower your upper body as you breathe in.
- Repeat to complete a set.

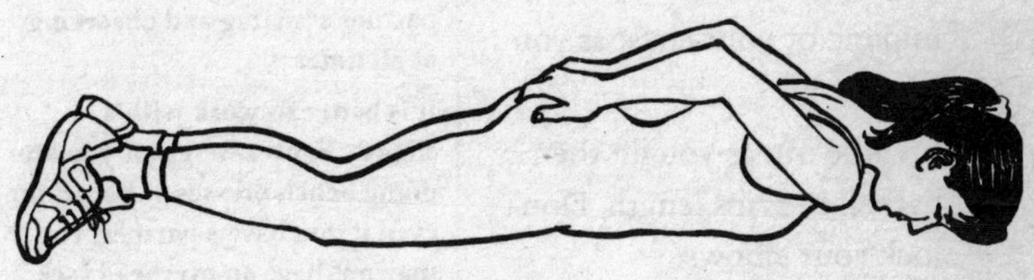

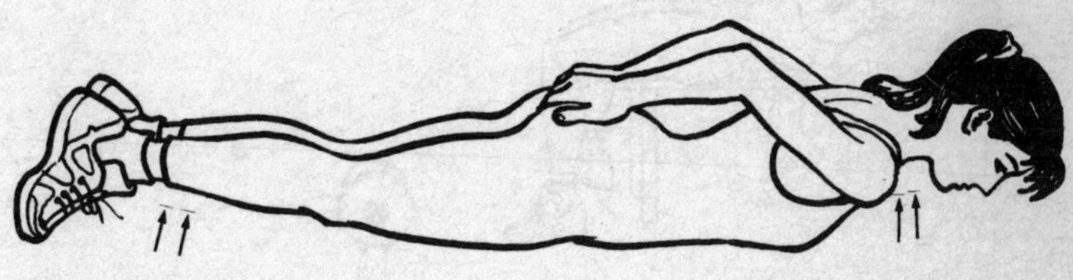

Flat Bench Press

Muscles worked: Pectorals, triceps and deltoids.

Recommended level: Beginners (Weeks 5 to 10).

- Lie down on the bench with your feet flat on the floor and hip-width apart.
- Grip the barbell with both hands, keeping the hands more than shoulder-width apart.
- Lower the barbell to the midlinc of your chest as you breathe in.
- Breathe out as you lift the barbell to arms length. Don't lock your elbows.
- Repeat to complete a set.

A word of caution

This exercise is best done if you have a special bench which has a rack to hold heavy weights. It is also advisable to do this exercise with a partner. A straight barbell is better than a pair of dumbbells.

You can do bench presses at home if you have a barbell and a partner. Sit down on the edge of a low settee or divan with a hard surface. Place the barbell on your thighs, and then lie down so that you are in the position described at the beginning of the exercise. Now gently ease the barbell towards your chest, have a partner assisting and observing at all times.

It is better to work with a slightly lighter weight if you are doing bench presses at home, for even if you have a partner, you may not have an overhead rack to hold the barbell.

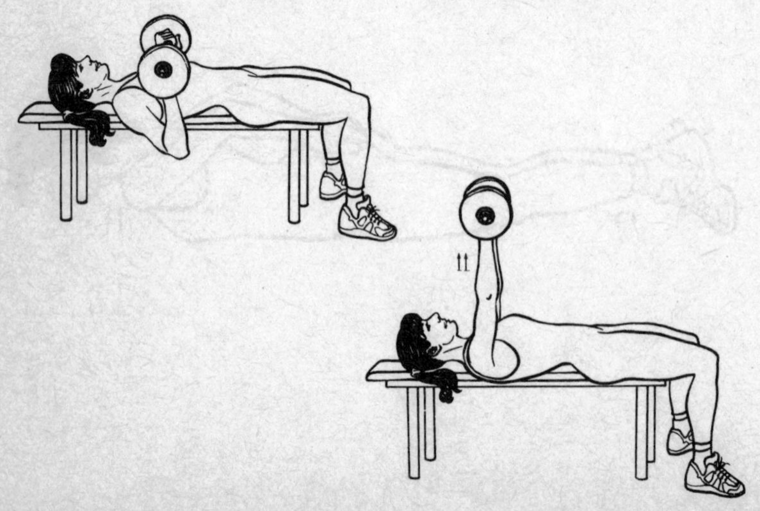

Advanced Lunges

Muscles worked: Quadriceps, hamstrings and gluteals.

Recommended level: Advanced.

- Follow the steps given for lunges on p. 131.
- Perform the lunges while carrying a pair of dumbbells by your sides, palms facing inward.
- Repeat to complete a set.

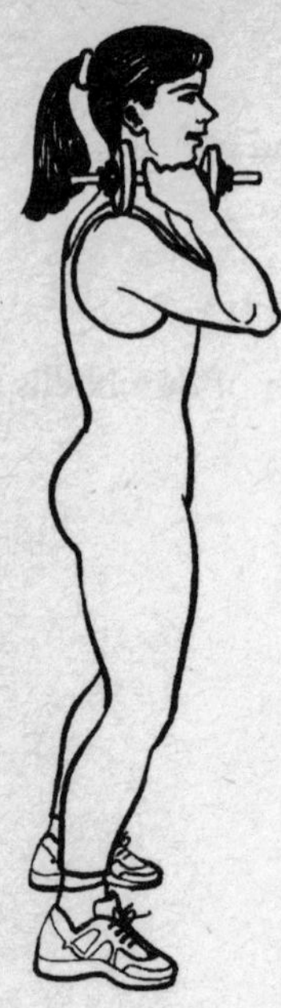

Advanced squats

Muscles worked:
Quadriceps, hamstrings and gluteals.

Recommended level:
Advanced.

- Follow the steps given for squats on p. 132.
- You can:
  (i) keep your arms outstretched or
  (ii) carry a pair of dumbbells at the level of your shoulders, with palms facing inward.
- Repeat to complete a set.

Upright Rows

Muscles worked: Trapezius, deltoids and triceps.

Recommended level: Advanced.

- Begin from the primary position.
- Dead lift a barbell to the front of the thighs. Your hands should be 4–6 inches apart.
- Breathe out as you draw the barbell up to your chest, as high as is comfortably possible. Keep the bar close to your body.
- Hold briefly.
- Lower to resting position.
- Repeat to complete a set.

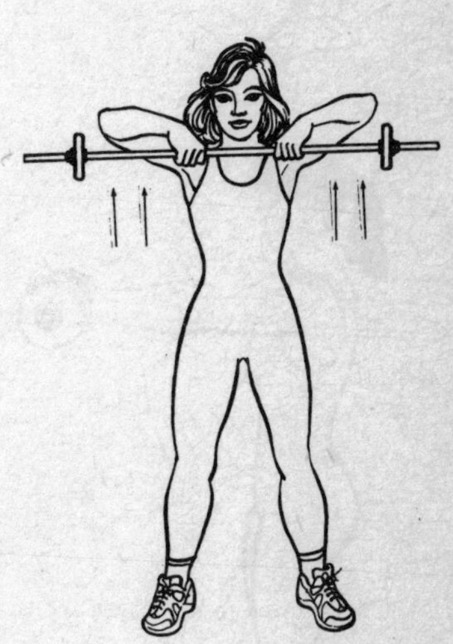

A word of caution

You can substitute a pair of dumbbells for a barbell. Use one in each hand, keeping the hands close together. Avoid swinging.

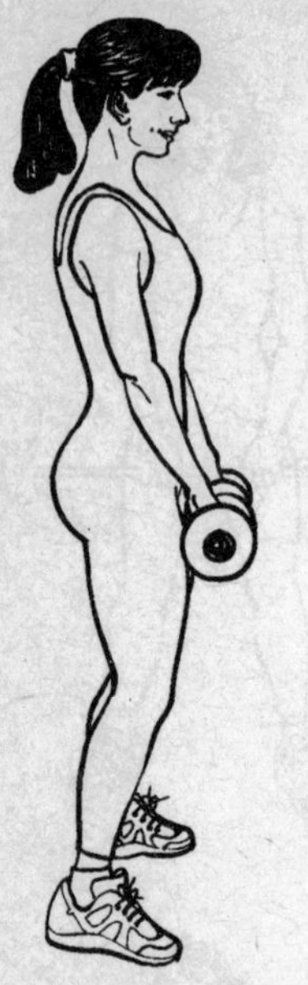

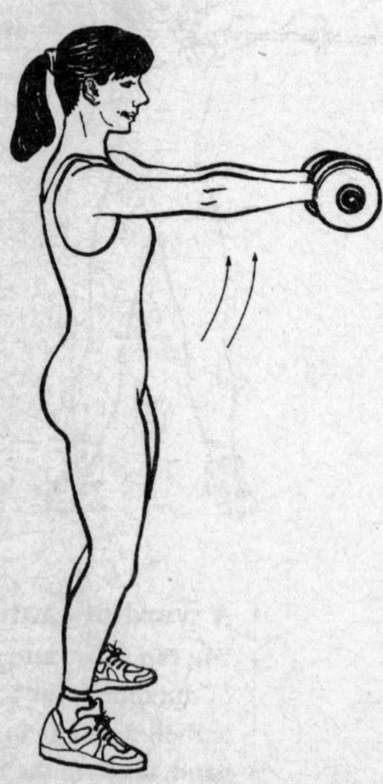

Forward Raise

Muscles worked: Pectorals and deltoids.

Recommended level: Advanced.

- Begin from the primary position.
- Lift a pair of dumbbells by your side, then bring them to the front of the thigh with the palms facing towards your body.
- Breathe out as you raise the dumbbells forward to shoulder height. Your palms should be facing downward when you complete this step.
- Hold briefly.
- Lower weights to resting position.
- Repeat to complete a set.

Shoulder Shrugs

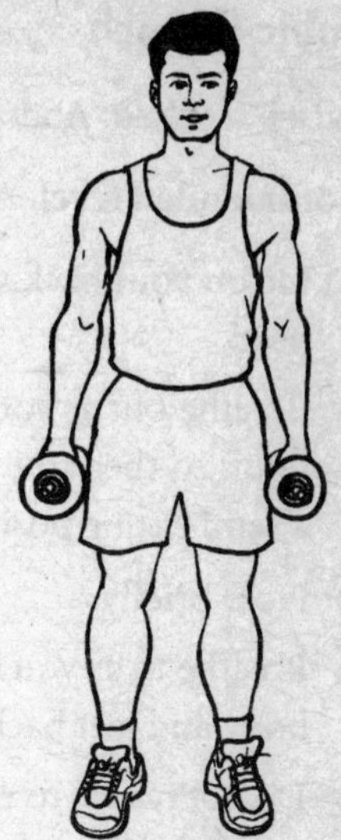

Muscles worked:
Rhomboids and trapezius.

Recommended level:
Advanced.

- Begin from the primary position.
- Dead lift a pair of dumbbells to your side, palms facing inward.
- Breathe out as you slowly raise your shoulders, then roll them back.
- Hold briefly when your shoulders are at the farthest point back.
- Breathe in as you return to resting position.
- Repeat to complete set.

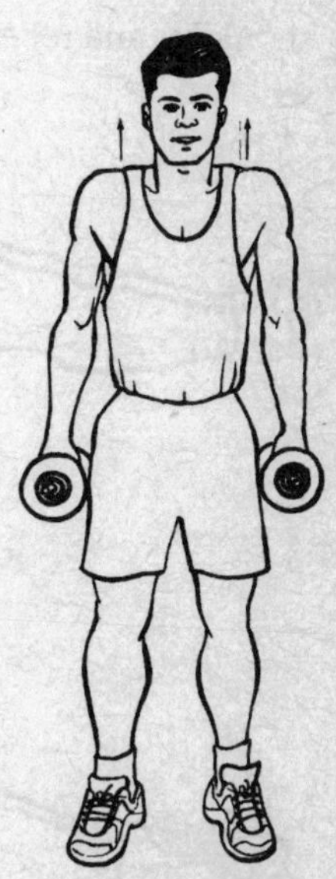

A word of caution
Keep the dumbbells close to the body at all times.

Double Crunch

Muscles worked: Abdominals.

Recommended level: Advanced.

- Lie on your back with feet together and hands under your head.
- Breathe out as you bend your knees and lift them off the floor. At the same time raise your shoulders so that you are in a semi-sitting position.
- Hold briefly.
- Breathe in as you lower your upper body and feet back to the floor.
- Do not return to resting position. Brush the floor with your feet and shoulders and repeat to complete a set.

A word of caution
This exercise is not recommended for those who have a weak back or abdomen. It is better to do this at the very end of your workout.

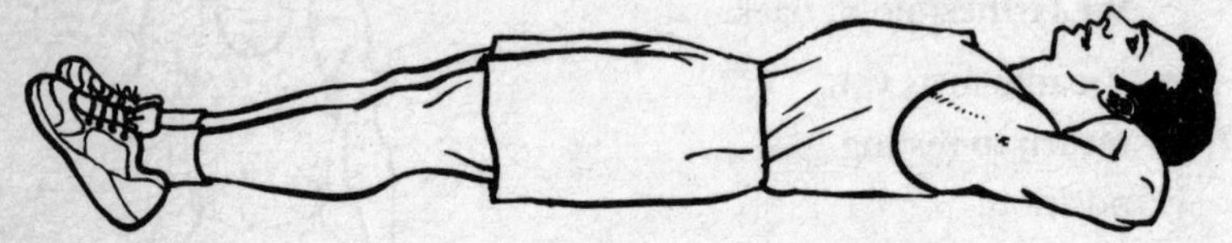

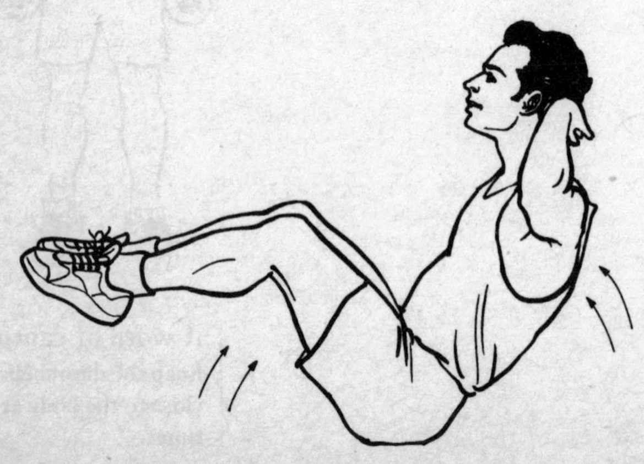

Bicycling

Muscles worked: Obliques and abdominals.

Recommended level: Advanced.

- Lie on your back on the floor with your hands under your head, elbows on the floor, knees bent and hip-width apart.
- Breathe out as you bend your left knee and draw it towards your chest. Keep your right leg pointing forward.
- Straighten out your left leg, and simultaneously bend your right knee and draw it towards your chest.
- Repeat to complete a set.

A word of caution

Keep your lower back on the floor during this exercise, and your abdominals contracted.

Exercises for Those with Special Needs

Exercise During Pregnancy

Many believe that if not absolute bed rest, then at least absence of any form of exertion should be the norm during pregnancy. This is not true. Barring certain conditions, most women should and do exercise during the gestation period. A number of pregnancy-related problems can be prevented by suitable exercise.

Because of the physiologic changes associated with pregnancy, as well as the haemodynamic response (relating to the flow of blood within the organs and tissues of the body) to exercise, some precautions should be observed. The physician should screen for any contraindications to exercise and encourage patients to avoid overly vigorous activity, especially in the third trimester, when most pregnant women have a decreased tolerance for weight-bearing activities. Pregnant women should avoid exercise that involves the risk of abdominal trauma, falls or excessive joint stress. In the absence of any obstetric or medical complications, most women can maintain a regular exercise regimen during pregnancy. The benefits of regular exercise for pregnant women are generally acknowledged.

A word of caution

It is crucially important that any exercise undertaken during pregnancy should be suitable to the person's need and should be undertaken after consultation with a doctor. Exercises need to be tailormade for each individual.

What are the benefits of exercise during pregnancy?

- **Increases feeling of well being**: Many pregnant women become physically unfit, lethargic, mentally dull, and may even sink into apathy at the prospect of nine months with a swollen body. Exercise makes a pregnant women feel better physically and leads to a feeling of well being which benefits both her and the baby.

- **Maintains healthy weight gain**: Women usually should put on about 9–11 kilograms during pregnancy. However many women put on much more than that. They may also develop high blood pressure and diabetes, and consequently have a more traumatic pregnancy. They also experience additional discomfort during labour. Regular exercise prevents excessive deposition of fat in the body. It also prevents water retention to some extent. By improving circulation, exercise prevents the problem of lower limb varicose veins and pregnancy piles.
- **Reduces pregnancy-related problems**: Backache, limb and joint pains, abdominal bloating and constipation are some of the common problems of pregnancy, which largely affect women with sedentary habits and can usually be prevented by exercising.
- **Reduces the chances of a complicated labour**: Unless there is some specific obstetric need, women who exercise regularly tend to have a smooth and uneventful labour. Some studies have shown decreased duration of labour in those who exercised regularly during pregnancy. Others have also shown less need for induction with uterine stimulants such as pitocin in such women, or for epidural analgesia or operative births.
- **Reduces recovery time after childbirth**: Recovery time after birth depends on one's fitness level. Those who exercise/sleep better, eat better, and have higher energy levels need less recovery time than those who do not. Postpartum weight loss is accelerated by exercise, and so is involution of the uterus to its pre-pregnant state.

What are the guidelines for exercise during pregnancy?

Pregnancy is a highly complex physiologic state, and you must always be very careful and consult your physician before you start or continue your existing exercise programme to ensure that this does not contribute to complications. Your individual medical and exercise history must be taken into consideration to see if you have any conditions which might restrict your physical activity during pregnancy. If you have no serious medical problems and you have an uncomplicated pregnancy, it is probably safe for you to do some exercising. You should plan the specific programme in consultation with your physician.

If you haven't exercised before, you need to start very slowly. If you have already been exercising, it's easier to continue during pregnancy.

If your doctor approves, you can start exercising at a level that does not cause pain, shortness of breath or excessive tiredness. You may then slowly increase your activity. If you feel uncomfortable, short of breath or very tired, you must reduce your exercise level.

Before you start, you need to take into account your pre-pregnancy fitness and activity level. Most physically fit women can continue most activities at or slightly below levels prior to pregnancy. Do not try to exceed pre-pregnancy levels.

- Regular, mild to moderate exercise, three times per week is preferable to an irregular schedule.
- Do not focus on great achievements. Exercise in moderation. Avoid competitive sports altogether. Do not take up a new, strenuous sport or try to increase your level of aerobic endurance.
- After the first trimester (from the fourth month onwards), avoid any exercise where you have to lie supine. In this position, the expanding uterus compresses the vein that carries blood to the heart, which could interfere with blood flow out of the heart and to the growing foetus.
- Exercise capabilities decline in pregnancy, so it is important to listen to your body. Your body will naturally give you signals that it is time to reduce the level of exercise you perform. Never exercise to the point of exhaustion or breathlessness. This is a sign that your baby and your body cannot get the oxygen supply they need. Avoid an anaerobic or breathless pace during exercise. Stop as soon as you feel fatigued.

- If you are used to a regimen of high-intensity aerobic activity, you should cut down the period you devote to these to a maximum of 10–15 minutes. Lower intensity activities may be practised continuously over a longer period but should not exceed 40 minutes in total.
- You should measure your heart rate during peak activity, and this should not exceed 140 beats per minute. One way to determine whether exercise is too intense is the 'talk test': if you are unable to converse normally while exercising, you are over-exerting yourself.
- Strenuous exercise should not be performed in hot, humid weather or during any illness accompanied by fever. Keep your body cool, especially in the first trimester, where there can be a risk of teratogenic changes (congenital malfunctions) in the foetus due to overheating. Your temperature should not exceed 100.4°F while exercising. You can minimize thermal stress by exercising early in the morning or late in the evening. If you are working out indoors, use fans or air conditioners to reduce room temperatures. Swimming may be an option to improve conductive heat loss. Hot tubs and sauna baths are not recommended. Do not exercise at all during an illness with fever.
- You should drink plenty of water before and after exercise to prevent dehydration and hypothermia. Take a break while exercising if more water is needed. Drinking up to one pint of liquid before exercising, and one cup of liquid every 20 minutes during exercise should be sufficient to maintain adequate hydration. Even if you are not thirsty after exercise, you should drink enough liquid to replenish lost fluids.
- All movements should be slow and gentle. Care should be taken to rise from the floor gradually to avoid an abrupt drop in blood pressure, and to continue some form of activity involving the legs for a brief period.
- Exercise sessions should be followed by a brief cool-down period of gradually declining activity that includes gentle stationary stretching. Stretches should not be taken to the maximum resistance, because the joints are already 'loosened' by the action

of a pregnancy hormone called relaxin. Too much stretching can be actually harmful.

- Choose exercises that do not require great balance because coordination and centre of gravity are changed. The weight of the baby becomes an important factor around the twentieth week of pregnancy. This increases instability and there is a greater risk of falls. All sports where there is a chance of falling should be avoided, as should those requiring sudden movement or balance. If you run, walk or cycle (this should perhaps be avoided) outdoors, avoid uneven or rocky terrain.
- Exercises that require jumping, jarring motions or rapid changes in direction should be avoided. These can cause damage to connective tissue.
- Avoid exercise with risk of even mild abdominal trauma, and all contact sports.
- Maintain an adequate diet. Pregnancy requires an additional 300 calories per day. Do not try to lose weight during pregnancy.
- If weight gain is not sufficient, it is a good idea to reduce the time or strenuousness of the regimen.
- Avoid prolonged Valsalva maneouvres (forced exhalation against closed mouth and nostrils while holding your breath), such as happens during lifting heavy weights, which can lead to an increase in blood pressure and can interfere with the blood flow to the heart. It results in decreases in splanchnic blood flow (blood flow of the viscera and internal organs, especially the abdomen) and uterine perfusion (supply of blood/blood substitutes to the uterus).
- Avoid prolonged periods of motionless standing. This position has not only been associated with decreased cardiac output, it is held by some authorities to be directly responsible for pregnancy piles and varicose veins.
- If you don't have the time or desire to start on a regular workout schedule, try adding a little more physical activity to your day. Housework, gardening, walking and playing with your children are examples of good ways to do this. Periods of activity lasting

at least 10 minutes several times a day can provide great health benefits.

- Pregnancy loosens your joints in preparation for giving birth. All the connective tissue in the body becomes more lax than normal. You become more flexible, but also more prone to sprains and strains. Be sure to warm up well before exercise. To help prevent injury, avoid deep flexion and extension of the joints
- If you lift weights, cut back the weight and increase the repetitions. And never, ever hold your breath while lifting weights, or grunt to help you lift more. Weight training should emphasize improving tone especially in the upper body and abdominal area. Avoid lifting weights above your head and using weights that strain the lower back muscles.

What exercises can you do?

Aerobics: Aerobic exercise forces the body to tap into its oxygen stores, and over a prolonged period of time, results in an increase in the body's oxygen storage capacity and the overall level of fitness. In addition to the physical benefits, aerobic exercise can help relieve stress, give you an overall sense of well being, and aid in regaining your pre-pregnancy shape after childbirth. Gentle aerobics are a good idea. Low impact aerobics are a better alternative to high impact aerobics. If you are attending antenatal classes, you would be told about exercises which will be beneficial for you throughout pregnancy. If you were doing aerobics classes before you became pregnant, you must now tell your instructor that you are pregnant so that your exercise routine can be modified. Do not try new exercises during pregnancy. Do not try too hard either.

Cycling: Cycling is acceptable in pregnancy, provided you can keep it within safety norms. An exercycle is the recommended option. Avoid rocky, irregular terrain, be careful of falls, and cycle in moderation. As your pregnancy progresses, your sense of balance gets altered and you will have to take extra care to ensure that you don't injure yourself.

Dancing: Slow, langorous dance movements have tremendous therapeutic value. As long as you don't make any jerky movements, dancing can be a very enjoyable form of exercise. Do not lose your balance or tire yourself to exhaustion

Jogging or running: If you have never jogged before, it may not be a good idea to start now. There is nothing to be gained by being over ambitious. Take things at a slow pace. Fast walking could be a better alternative. If you have been jogging before pregnancy, you may need to decrease both speed and distance.

Racquet sports: Tennis, squash and badminton can put an undue strain on the joints due to jerky and sudden movements. Injuries to the tendons and ligaments can actually increase during pregnancy. Loss of balance and falls are common, especially in the last three months. If at all you want to, avoid any kind of competition. Be very careful while playing, if you must. Do some gentle practice instead.

Rowing: Pregnancy is not the time for beginners to learn rowing. Rowing can be extremely harmful to the lower back in pregnancy, if not done correctly. You can continue to row only if you were an expert rower before you became pregnant.

Stretching: Stretching is highly recommended in pregnancy. It is non-strenuous, extremely beneficial for relaxation and body toning. However, extra care needs to be taken not to overstretch the muscles in later pregnancy. Most antenatal classes teach you good stretching techniques. If you haven't joined a class, most pregnancy books have some exercises that you can carry out safely at home.

Swimming and water exercises: Swimming can be very relaxing in pregnancy because of the feeling of weightlessness, as the water supports your weight. Some places have aquatic classes designed specially for pregnant women. Ask your club for details. Water aerobics gives you a great workout without putting stress on your body. However certain moves, such as stomach crunches, aren't safe if you're pregnant. Also, bouncing or jumping out of the water can lead to muscle strain and back problems. Most water exercises provide a good, low impact workout, and can be started during pregnancy.

Volleyball, softball and basketball: These are better avoided as immense trauma could be caused by a direct hit to the abdomen.

Walking: This is an extremely safe and gentle form of exercise, more so in late pregnancy when many women find any kind of movement challenging as the body gets totally imbalanced. This and the sheer increase in weight may prevent you from doing any other form of exercise.

A word of caution

The following activities should be avoided during pregnancy due to increased risk to the mother and/or baby.

- **competitive sports**
- **snow skiing**
- **hang gliding**
- **springboard diving**
- **horseback riding**
- **volleyball, softball and basketball**
- **scuba diving**
- **water skiing**
- **sky diving**

Weight training: Pregnancy is associated with a tendency to back injuries. Therefore, weight training becomes all the more dangerous. However, if you must, use light weights. Work out sensibly, substituting increased sets and reps for increase in weights, and under the guidance of a professional.

Yoga: Yoga is great for relaxation, suppleness, breathing control and developing concentration. You can either join yoga classes or pick gentle yoga exercises from books.

How should you modify the 20-minute plan to suit pregnancy?

It is important to remember the following:

- **Flexibility regarding time**. You have to make concessions to your pregnancy. Set your own pace while doing the exercises. Nothing is to be gained by rushing through it. You may find it difficult to complete the workout in the very first attempt. In that case, start with as many exercises as you can perform comfortably, then add one exercise every week, till you are able to complete the full quota.
- **Maintaining the right posture**. Your centre of gravity changes during pregnancy. Avoid the temptation to slump forward. Stand erect, with your eyes facing forward, head held high, chin tucked in and your neck straight. Lift your shoulders and pull them back. If you have to sit down, choose a straight-backed chair rather than a soft cushioned seat where you would sink low into the cushions. Keep your back straight. Do not slump forward. Rest your thighs along the length of the chair. Place a pillow behind the small of your

back, if so desired. If you have to sit on the floor, sit cross-legged (also called the tailor position). This has its own benefits. It stretches and increases flexibility along the inner thigh muscles. Avoid lying supine. Lying on your side, especially in the left lateral position, increases blood supply to the foetus and promotes growth. To get up from the bed, roll onto the side, and prop yourself up on your arms. Now get up slowly.

PREGNANCY MENU

Time	*Category*	*Exercises*	*Notes*
3 minutes daily	Warm up	Rib cage stretch Arm circles Shoulder rolls (see p. 116)	Do each exercise only for 1 minute.
4 minutes daily	Stretching	Neck Stretch (see p. 120) Triceps stretch (see p. 122) Calf stretch (see p. 127) Total body stretch (see p. 128)	Do each exercise only for 1 minute.
5 minutes daily	Pregnancy-specific exercise	Pelvic rock Tailor press Isometric tailor press Tailor stretch Pelvic tilt	Do each exercise only for 1 minute. In addition you should do Kegel exercises throughout the day.
5 minutes on alternate days	Aerobics		
	Light weight training	Biceps curls Triceps curls Back raise Wall press up Beginners squats	
3 minutes daily	Cool down	Continue with your aerobic activity or repeat the stretching exercises	

Rib Cage Stretch

- Stand in the basic position.
- Inhale slowly while raising your arms over head. Do this slowly to a count of five.
- Exhale, while lowering your arms down. Move your arms gradually first to the front, then downwards and backwards, as far back as comfortable. Count to five while lowering the arms.
- Do this as many times as you can in a minute.

A word of caution

Do not arch your back or lean forward while taking your arms backward.

Arm Circles

- Stand in the basic position.
- Stretch your arms to your sides with the palms facing upwards.
- Make small circles, gradually increasing the size of the circles.
- Reverse the direction of the circles, starting with large circles, and gradually decreasing the size of the circles till you reach the stretched out arms position.
- Return to basic position

Pelvic Rock

Benefits: Improves posture, relieves back discomfort, and makes labour a little easier.

- Kneel on the floor on your hands and knees. Keep your spine straight.
- Pull up the abdominal muscles and tighten the buttocks.
- Hold for 4–5 seconds, then return to starting position.
- Repeat.

If you are hesitant in going down to the kneeling position, you can do the exercise standing up. Stand in front of a mirror. Place one hand on the pubic bone and another at the small of the back. Tuck in your bottom and abdomen, this will rotate your pelvis forward. Relax and repeat, using a rocking motion.

Tailor Press

Benefits: Relaxes the muscles on the inner aspects of the thigh. This helps while giving birth.

- Sit on the floor in the tailor position, with your legs in front of you, the soles of your feet pressed together and pulled as close to the body as is comfortably possible.
- Hold your ankles gently.
- Using the muscles of the thighs, press your knees downwards towards the floor.
- Hold for 6–10 seconds.
- Repeat.

A word of caution

Do not do this exercise if you have pain around the public bone. Do not do this exercise until six weeks after delivery, or till the perineum has healed.

Isometric Tailor Press

Benefits: Relaxes the muscles on the inner aspects of the thigh. This helps while giving birth.

- Sit on the floor in the tailor position, as for the previous exercise.
- Place hands on the knees.
- Try to pull the knees up with your hands, while trying to push them down using the thigh muscles.
- Hold for 6–10 seconds.
- Now try to push the knees with your hands, while trying to pull them up using the thigh muscles.
- Hold for 6–10 seconds.
- Repeat.

A word of caution

Do not do these exercises if you have pain around the pubic bone. After delivery, do not do these for six weeks after delivery, or till the perineum has healed.

Tailor Stretch

Benefits: Relaxes the muscles on the inner aspects of the thigh. This helps while giving birth.

- Sit on the floor with the legs stretched out. Separate the legs at a wide angle.
- Place hands on the knees.
- Lean forward and slide your hands down the legs, as far towards the ankle as possible.
- Hold for 5 seconds.
- Repeat.

Pelvic Tilt

- Lie down on the floor.
- Bend your knees and keep your feet flat on the floor.
- Inhale deeply.
- While exhaling, lift your tail bone upwards towards the naval, keeping your hips pressed to the ground.
- Tighten your buttocks and abdominals.
- Hold for 5 seconds.
- Release and repeat.

What exercises should you do to prepare for labour?

- Prior to delivery many physicians recommend doing pelvic floor exercises (Kegel exercises) to strengthen the muscles needed to push during the delivery.
- Breathing exercises.
- Other recommendations include pelvic tilt exercises to help avoid the lower back pain that frequently accompanies pregnancy in the later stages.

What are Kegel exercises?

These exercises were developed by Dr Arnold Kegel. They restore or improve the tone of the muscles of the pelvic floor. These muscles form sphincters around the urethra, vagina and anus, and strengthen control of these.

During childbirth, the pelvic floor gets stretched, and these muscles get bruised or torn and devitalized. This can cause problems such as sagging or prolapse of the genital organs, stress incontinence (leakage of urine caused by anything that raises the intra-abdominal pressure, such as coughing or sneezing), and prolapse of the walls of the bladder and rectum.

Kegel exercises prevent stress incontinence and prolapse, increase blood flow to the perineum which aids in early healing, and tighten the vaginal orifice and thereby increase sexual pleasure.

- Identify the muscles which constitute the pelvic floor. In order to do this, try and stop the flow of urine while micturating. Stopping the flow tightens the pelvic floor. Do this several times till you are sure of which muscle you have to tighten.
- Once you have identified the muscles, practice this exercise after passing urine, on an empty bladder.
- Lift and tighten the muscles of the pelvic floor and hold for 20 seconds.

- Do this exercise 10–20 times a day.
- Continue the exercise in the postpartum period, and throughout your life.

What breathing exercises should you do?

These should be practised in the third trimester, from the seventh month onwards. Your partner should participate in these exercises.

These are an important part of your antenatal preparation. If done properly, breathing exercises will help you greatly when labour pains begin. You will ensure a good oxygen supply to the uterus, avoid harmful attacks of hyperventilation, your perception of pain will decrease and you will require less analgesia. Determine your respiratory rate (the number of times you breathe in a minute) before you start.

What is the relaxing breath?

Take a smooth, deep breath through the nose. Then exhale through the mouth. The air should escape like a sigh. The relaxing breath should be done at the beginning and the end of every contraction. In between—during the contraction—practise your breathing pattern. Focus on some object or spot in the room (the focal point) during the pain, or close your eyes and mentally focus on a pleasing thought.

What is slow-paced breathing?

Slow paced breathing should be done as long as possible during labour.

- Take a relaxing breath.
- Breathe slowly, at half your normal rate.
- Focus on your focal point while breathing.
- Repeat the relaxing breath at the end of the pain.

What is modified paced breathing?

This should be done when slow-paced breathing no longer gives you comfort.

- Take a relaxing breath.
- Breathe faster (rate should vary from half to twice the respiratory rate).
- Concentrate on your focal point.
- Repeat the relaxing breath.
- If you are hyperventilating, re-breathe into your cupped hands. This will slow down your respiratory rate by increasing the carbon dioxide content of the inhaled air.

What is patterned-paced breathing?

This should be done when modified paced breathing is no longer effective, usually towards the end of labour during strong contractions.

- Take a relaxing breath.
- Take three or four shallow breaths, then blow out (as if you are blowing out a candle) with pursed lips.
- Repeat the relaxing breath.

What breathing exercises should you do to prevent premature pushing?

If you feel the urge to push, but your doctor says it is too early to do so, blow out repeatedly and forcefully through the mouth till the urge passes. You cannot bear down effectively while you are blowing out.

How should you modify your weight-training programme?

You might feel uncomfortable while doing exercises which involve lying on the back. If you feel dizzy, lightheaded or nauseous, discontinue.

For beginners' squats, stand against a wall. This will give support to the back. Slide your back down the wall till you reach an imaginary sitting position.

For dumbbell exercises, start with 500-gram weights. Initially do 1 set of eight to ten reps, with a pause between reps. When you can do three to five sets easily, increase the weight by 500 grams.

Do not pick up weights if your back hurts or if you feel sore anywhere.

When should you not exercise?

There are many reasons to not exercise in pregnancy. If you have any of the following problems, avoid exercise all together.

- **Toxemia**: Toxemia or high blood pressure that develops during pregnancy is thought to involve a severe problem with blood vessels throughout the body. Exercise can worsen this and so should be discontinued.
- **Vaginal bleeding** or pain in the first three months: This does not necessarily mean that a miscarriage is about to take place, but that is one possibility. Rest is one way to stop uterine cramps. Stop exercise immediately if you are experiencing first trimester pain or bleeding.
- **Placenta previa** or late vaginal bleeding: Placenta previa is a condition where the placenta grows low in the uterus and may actually cover the opening to the cervix. It can cause severe bleeding during pregnancy, which is typically described as painless and causeless. Exercise can precipitate an attack of haemorrhage. If you have a placenta previa, or if you have had vaginal bleeding due to any cause, you should not exercise.
- **History of pre-term labour**: If you have previously delivered a baby before thirty-six weeks of pregnancy, you should be very cautious about exercising during the second and third trimesters. Stretching, yoga and walking are the recommended forms of exercise, if at all, while weight-bearing exercise should be avoided. If you have pre-term contractions, you should strictly avoid all exercise. It has been found that exercise stimulates the release of hormones such as norepinephrine in the body, that can augment or initiate uterine contractions.
- **Intra-uterine growth retardation**: IUGR is a condition where the foetus does not grow adequately, and is diagnosed by your physician by measuring the growth of your uterus and by checking a foetal sonogram. The growth of the baby depends on the blood supply across the placenta, and IUGR indicates inadequate supply. As exercise shifts the blood flow away from the placenta, it should be avoided in all cases of IUGR.

- **Multiple pregnancy**: If you are pregnant with more than one foetus, you have a higher risk of complications of pregnancy such as pre-term labour. Rest is imperative in such cases. Exercise, if at all, should be limited to non-weight-bearing ones and should focus on toning and stretching. Multiple pregnancies lead to over-distension of the uterus and may raise and splint the diaphragm even more than usual, so breathing exercises are recommended.
- **Heart disease**: Pregnancy increases the strain on the heart. If you have a history of heart disease , and are pregnant, exercise should be done, if at all, under the supervision of a cardiologist. (*See section on exercise and heart disease*.)
- **Premature rupture of membranes**: Sometimes during pregnancy, the bag of water can start leaking or even burst. This is a condition that can very well lead to premature labour. Stop all exercise if you are suffering from PROM.
- **Incompetent cervix or circlage**: Incompetent cervix is the name given to the condition where the mouth of the uterus is so weak that the baby may slip out any time after the first trimester. This condition is treated by putting a strengthening stitch or circlage on the cervix. Bed rest is a must for such patients.
- **Chronic hypertension** (high blood pressure).
- Active thyroid, heart, vascular, metabolic (i.e. diabetes) or lung diseases.

A word of caution

You should stop exercising right away and call your physician if you have any of the following symptoms:

- **Breathlessness**
- **Dizziness**
- **Headaches**
- **Muscle weakness**
- **Nausea**
- **Chest pain or tightness**
- **Uterine contractions**
- **Vaginal bleeding**
- **Water loss through the vagina**
- **Sudden swelling anywhere in the body**
- **Pain in the vagina**
- **Palpitations**
- **Pain in the back, knees or any other joint**

What exercises should you do after delivering?

Most women are very eager to regain their pre-pregnancy figures, and women who have exercised throughout their pregnancy will find this much easier than those who haven't exercised during this period.

As with all exercise programmes when you were first pregnant, you need to start off slowly. You may only start exercising again once your body has completely healed from the stress of labour.

Return to pre-pregnancy routines gradually. It takes four to six weeks to recover after a vaginal delivery, and ten to twelve weeks after a Caesarian section.

Exercising with Medical Conditions

Asthma

Traditionally asthmatics were discouraged from exercising as it was believed that this could cause acute breathlessness. However, it has been proved beyond doubt that regular exercise is not only beneficial, it is very much an integral part of asthma treatment. Exercise, with all its accompanying benefits of increased lung capacity, results in a decrease in the number of acute asthmatic episodes, with a resultant improvement in health and productivity.

What exercises should you do?

You should choose an aerobic activity that is easy and enjoyable; walking, slow jogging, biking and swimming. These activities are steady, therefore less likely to provoke symptoms.

An alternative would be to substitute aerobics with sports that involve short bursts of intense activity, like tennis, badminton or basketball.

You should avoid strenuous weight training. If your asthma is well controlled, you can work out with light weights, giving yourself plenty of time between sets. Stop immediately if you feel an attack coming on.

MODIFIED BEGINNERS' MENU		
Weeks 1 and 2	5 minutes	Warm up
	Maximum 5 minutes	Aerobic activity (depending on exercise tolerance)
	5 minutes	Cool down
Weeks 3 and 4	5 minutes	Warm up
	5 minutes	Aerobic activity (depending on exercise tolerance)
	Maximum 5 minutes	Light weights (maximum weight 500 grams)
	5 minutes	Cool down
Week 5 onwards	Increase aerobic activity to a maximum of 15 minutes. Keep weight training to 5 minutes, but you can gradually increase weights if you are comfortable.	

What precautions should you take?

Even if your asthma is well controlled, you may develop symptoms during exercise. You can get shortness of breath, cough, chest pain, or nausea if you exercise without taking precautions. Several simple steps can prevent this exercise-induced asthma:

- Control your disease. Follow your doctor's advice before you get started. Do not exercise while you are suffering from dyspnoea (breathlessness).
- Take two puffs of an inhaler half an hour before exercising. (*Note: Do not self-medicate. Consult your doctor.*)
- Exercise for 20 minutes or less. Better still, break up your exercise into smaller capsules.
- Warm up before exercise.
- Stop if you feel an attack coming on. Take your treatment immediately.
- If you develop symptoms during exercise, don't force yourself to continue. You will be doing more harm than good. Stop what

you're doing and take your medication. If this doesn't bring relief within a few minutes, seek medical help.

- Do not exercise in cold dry air. During winter, it is a good idea to exercise indoors. Keep the temperature comfortably warm. Do not overheat the room.
- Check humidity. Switch on the humidifier before you start. Alternately, you could boil a kettle in your room. This will provide the necessary moisture in the inhaled air.
- Protect yourself from the cold. Wear several thin layers instead of one heavy woollen jacket. Discard as you get warmed up.
- Treat yourself for allergies. Avoid allergens or allergy provoking substances.
- Do not exercise on days when your symptoms are bothering you, or if you have recently recovered from a wheezing episode or an attack of chest infection.

Osteoarthritis

Exercise is an essential element of the treatment for arthritis. Regular exercise helps control pain, stiffness and other symptoms. The right kind of exercise will benefit the joints that have been damaged by osteoarthritis, leading to increased power, range of movement and flexibility. It also boosts your overall energy and ability to enjoy your favourite activities. Different kinds of exercise—aerobic, strengthening, flexibility, and specific joint exercises—can improve your health in different ways., and let you live a more vigorous, satisfying life.

As patients of osteoarthritis have chronically inflamed joints, all exercise has to be careful and controlled.

What exercises should you do?

Aerobic exercises raise your heart rate, strengthen your heart and lung power, and help break the vicious cycle of pain, stiffness and inactivity. Prevention of disability is therefore one of the main benefits of aerobic exercise. Depending on the joints involved, swimming, walking, cycling and water exercises that are easy on the damaged joints, are often the best exercises for people with osteoarthritis. You should do about 20 minutes of exercise regularly.

Regular physiotherapy is part of the treatment for osteoarthiritis. This includes active and passive joint movements, hot and cold packs, and ultrasound treatment. In acute attacks, all exercises are prohibited. When pain and inflammation begin to subside, exercise should begin. Start gently and gradually to prevent trauma and maximize movement around an affected joint.

Strength and flexibility training is also recommended. Lifting light weights helps arthritic patients. One of the problems all such patients expect is the loss of muscle mass and decreased muscle tone around the affected joint. Weight training reverses this process by building muscle throughout the body. Stretching keeps you supple, and gets rid of stiffness. It increases flexibility so that subsequent aerobic or anaerobic exercises become easy. Ask your doctor or physiotherapist about a full-body strength and flexibility workout.

MODIFIED BEGINNERS' MENU		
Weeks 1 and 2	5 minutes	Warm up
	Maximum 5 minutes	Aerobic activity (depending on exercise tolerance)
	5 minutes	Cool down
Weeks 3 and 4	5 minutes	Warm up
	5 minutes	Aerobic activity (depending on exercise tolerance)
	Maximum 5 minutes	Light weights (maximum weight 500 grams)
	5 minutes	Cool down
Week 5 onwards	Increase aerobic activity to a maximum of 15 minutes. Keep strength training to 5 minutes, but you can gradually increase weights if you are comfortable.	

What precautions should you take?

- Do not exercise in the acute phase. Your doctor might advise you to rest and give you some treatment in the form of medicines and cold packs.

- Start slowly. If you're out of shape, exercise for no more than 5 minutes at a time. (Even 2 minutes is fine.) Rest between sessions. Do this several times a day if you can.
- Build up gradually. Increase the length of your sessions by 10 per cent each week. If you are walking for 5 minutes a day, make it 6 minutes after a week.
- Challenge yourself, but don't push too hard. The idea is to get your heart pumping harder than usual. You may be a little out of breath, but you should be able to carry on a conversation while you work out.
- Maintain a healthy body weight. Carrying extra body weight can make your joints wear out faster. Even losing a few pounds leads to much less strain on the arthritic joint. Exercise, combined with healthy eating, is the best strategy for successful, permanent weight loss.
- Warm up before starting. This is an important component of exercise sessions, more so in arthritics where muscles surrounding the inflamed joint are stiff, sore or flabby due to prolonged disuse.
- Applying ice to your arthritic joint for 15–20 minutes after a workout will reduce soreness and help prevent swelling.
- Be prepared for minor discomforts. Some muscle ache or minor joint discomfort after exercise is normal. But if your joints are more painful for the next few days, suspend your workouts. Visit your doctor at the earliest.

Osteoporosis

Osteoporosis means that your bones do not have enough calcium in them, and are brittle, fragile and prone to fractures with trivial trauma. There are many factors that predispose a person to osteoporosis. Those who have a diet that has been chronically deficient in calcium are liable to suffer from this disease, as well as those who lead a sedentary lifestyle. Exercise mobilizes calcium into the bones. In women, oestrogen levels are required to maintain bone mass. After menopause, osteoporosis can set in easily, and it is more likely to occur if menopause has occurred early, or if the ovaries have been removed or irradiated.

For patients who have osteoporosis, exercise is most certainly part of the treatment. Regular workouts not only build muscle, they also maintain and increase bone density and strength. By strengthening the bones, improving your coordination and balance, and making muscles toned and powerful, exercise can reduce the risk of falls and resulting fractures.

Exercise works well with oestrogen or other medications that increase bone density and strength.

What exercises should you do?

Brisk walking is ideal, but avoid jogging and sprinting. Low-impact aerobic activities are recommended. Cycling, swimming and water exercises are safe.

Weight training exercises are strongly to be recommended. Lifting weights or using weight-training machines strengthens bones all over your body, especially if you exercise all the major muscle groups in your legs, arms and trunk. Strength training is a slow process, so start at a low level and build up gradually over several months. It is best to start with 500-gram weights. Remember your bones are brittle, and may snap with strenuous effort. Always select light weights. Do 1 set of 10–15 reps. As muscles strengthen, gradually add more weight. Do not increase the weight more than 10 per cent every week as a larger increase can raise the risk of injury. Remember to lift with good technique. Never sacrifice good technique for more weight.

What precautions should you take?

- You should be careful to start slowly, warm up properly, and cool off gradually after working out.
- When you are doing weights, lift and lower weights slowly to maximize muscle strength and minimize the risk of injury.

MODIFIED BEGINNERS' MENU		
Weeks 1 and 2	5 minutes	Warm up
	Maximum 5 minutes	Aerobic activity (depending on exercise tolerance)
	5 minutes	Cool down
Weeks 3 and 4	5 minutes	Warm up
	5 minutes	Aerobic activity (depending on exercise tolerance)
	Maximum 5 minutes	Light weights (maximum weight 500 grams)
	5 minutes	Cool down
Week 5 onwards	Increase aerobic activity to a maximum of 15 minutes. Keep strength training to 5 minutes, but you can gradually increase weights if you are comfortable.	

- It is best to perform your resistance workout every third day. This gives your body a chance to recover.
- Avoid exercise that puts excessive stress on your bones, such as running or high-impact aerobics.
- Avoid rowing machines—they require deep forward bending that may lead to a vertebral fracture.
- Stiffness the morning after exercise is normal. But if you're in pain most of the following day, your joints are swollen, or you're limping, stop the programme until you feel normal again, and cut your weights and reps by 25–50 per cent.
- If bone, joint or muscle pain is severe, call your doctor.
- If a particular area of your body feels sore right after exercise, apply ice for 10–15 minutes.

Heart disease

The term heart disease encompasses a group of disorders that can affect the heart, either directly or indirectly. Some common forms are:

- **Congenital heart disease** exists from birth, and is seen usually in small children. The degree of cardiac disability varies, and the child can be recommended anything between full bed rest and reasonably normal activity. Your cardiologist should recommend an activity level.

- **Ischemic heart disease** is the condition where the arteries supplying blood to the cardiac muscle get clogged with fat deposits, leading to ischemic pain. It is also called coronany artery disease.
- **Congestive heart disease** is when the heart becomes sluggish and malfunctioning.

These, as well as other cardiac conditions, require careful and scientific counselling regarding exercise.

Congestive heart disease

For many years, patients who had congestive heart failure (CHF) were advised to avoid physical activity. Bed rest was considered integral to the treatment. Now however it is accepted that mild to moderate exercise, done in a controlled manner, will benefit most CHF patients, and with little risk. Regular exercise acts synergistically with medication. It helps relieve symptoms due to a sluggish heart, such as shortness of breath and weakness. It enables patients to fend for themselves; those on regular exercise are able to manage their day to day business of living with minimal help from others. Exercise leads to independence. It prevents or limits other health problems like coronary heart disease, diabetes, high blood pressure and high cholesterol.

What exercises should you do?

Walking is one of the best options, being easy on the heart. A sample menu could consist of a 2-minute walk, followed by a minute of rest, repeated till 10 minutes of exercise have been achieved. Gradually, every week or so, you can increase the duration of exercise and decrease the interval of rest. The best exercises for CHF are aerobic activities, like walking or biking slowly.

Light weights help to develop power in the trunk and limbs.

Respiratory muscle exercises to build up your chest, diaphragm and abdominal muscles to help you breathe better.

Ideally, you should exercise for 20 minutes 3–5 times a week.

MODIFIED BEGINNERS' MENU		
Weeks 1 and 2	5 minutes	Warm up (with rest intervals as required)
	Maximum 5 minutes	Aerobic activity (depending on exercise tolerance and with rest intervals)
	5 minutes	Cool down
Weeks 3 and 4	5 minutes	Warm up
	5 minutes	Aerobic activity (depending on exercise tolerance and with rest intervals)
	Maximum 5 minutes	Light weights (maximum weight 500 grams)
	5 minutes	Cool down
Week 5 onwards	Increase aerobic activity to a maximum of 15 minutes. Keep weight training to 5 minutes, but you can gradually increase weights if you are comfortable.	

What precautions should you take?

- Visit a cardiologist before you start exercise.
- Take a stress test to see how your body responds to exercise. This will also help you to determine a safe, effective level of exercise.
- The vital point is starting slowly, especially if you have been inactive for a long time.
- Start with interval training, in which you exercise for a few minutes and then rest. This alternating pattern gives you the benefits of exercise without undue strain. Gradually you can increase the time and pace as you grow stronger.
- Be prepared for setbacks. Initially, you may develop a little swelling on the feet.

- Be alert for symptoms like chest pain, increasing shortness of breath, palpitations, weight gain, ankle swelling, abdominal bloating. Call your doctor, and stop exercising until the symptoms are controlled.

Ischemic heart disease

Exercise is vital if you've had angina pain or a full-fledged heart attack. Exercise, with lifestyle modifications, has significantly improved prognosis after all kinds of heart surgery such as balloon angioplasty or bypass surgery. Regular physical activity under your doctor's direction is a key part of managing your disease.

Patients find that increased physical activity boosts their confidence, increases their fitness level, and reduces chances of further heart attacks. After angina or myocardial infarction, depression, stress, and social isolation are common and all can be decreased to a large extent by regular exercise.

Some people worry about having a heart attack while exercising. While the risk is a bit higher during a workout than while resting, this can be minimized by being careful. Most cardiologists believe that those heart patients who do not exercise have a greater risk of ischemic heart disease than those who are active. Inactive people are at a higher overall risk of a heart attack than those who exercise regularly.

What exercises should you do?

One of the most important components of an exercise programme for heart patients is aerobic exercise. Walking is considered the best, but all other aerobic activities are as fruitful. Regularity and consistency are necessary ingredients of a successful exercise plan. You should do something you enjoy doing, otherwise compliance will suffer. Because aerobic exercise stresses your heart, get clearance from a doctor before you start. This is even more important if you are very inactive, overweight, middle-aged or elderly. Medical clearance is also important if you have several other risk factors for heart disease, like smoking, high cholesterol, high blood pressure, diabetes, or a family history of heart disease.

Variety in your workouts can help you adhere to your exercise programme. If you enjoy walking, adding variety may simply mean changing your route from time to time or exercising with a friend.

You may want to try another type of exercise, like jogging, biking, dancing, swimming or aerobics classes. Exercise machines like stationary bikes, cross-country ski machines, stair-climbing machines, treadmills and rowing machines also provide good cardiovascular workouts.

Interval training is a good option.

To allow weight training or not has been the dilemma faced by cardiologists over the years. It has now been found that weight training helps improve the physical condition. In addition to increasing your muscle fitness and well being, gradual and sustained weight training can reduce the heart-rate and blood-pressure responses to strenuous work. Thus, resistance training can decrease the demands on your heart during day-to-day activities, both at work and at leisure.

Heavy loads, however, can place undue stress on the heart, so use light loads that permit a lot of reps (ideally 10–15) per set.

Weight training should work all the major muscle groups in your body. High volume, low intensity exercises are best for cardiac patients. Do all exercises using very light weights. Increase sets and reps rather than weights.

(See modified beginners' menu on p. 184.)

What precautions should you take?

- It is important to fix the level of activity. Find out from your doctor what is the heart rate at which symptoms of breathlessness or chest pain start occurring. This can very easily be done in a hospital using a treadmill. Once this has been found out, your aim should be to exercise in such a manner that the heart rate stays 10 beats less than that which produces symptoms.

- Warming up properly is very important. Prepare your muscles and raise your heart rate gradually by doing calisthenics and stretching for 5–10 minutes. After your workout, cool down by walking and stretching for at least 5 minutes.
- Work out at a moderate intensity. You should be breathing hard while exercising, but not gasping for breath.
- Watch out for the warning signs of imminent cardiac crisis. At the slightest feeling of discomfort in the chest, back or limbs, stop immediately. Do not wait for actual pain. Be alert for other symptoms such as breathlessness, palpitations, dizziness, nausea and sweating.
- Watch out for abnormal heart rhythm. Irregular heart beats, called arrhythmias, feel like extra heart beats or skipped beats.
- Pain or pressure in the centre of your chest during or after exercise is an ominous sign. It means that your heart muscle is not getting enough oxygen. The pain may radiate across your chest or down the left arm. Pain or pressure in your back, throat or stomach may also be a warning sign.
- Dizziness during or just after exercise may be a symptom of a serious circulation problem.
- Unusual tiredness during or after exercise can be a heart-related symptom.

High blood pressure

High blood pressure is a potentially life-threatening condition, which may well lead to even more serious problems such as heart attacks or paralytic strokes. Regular exercise, especially aerobic exercise, has been found to be effective in lowering blood pressure significantly.

The immediate response to exercise, though, is to raise the blood pressure a little. This happens because the body diverts blood to working muscles. Although this effect is only temporary, it can prove risky to those who have severe hypertension. It is best that your doctor lower your BP through medication before you increase your physical activity. Exercise for people who have mild or moderate hypertension, however, is generally safe.

What exercises should you do?

Walking is the safest and simplest option, far better than high intensity exercises such as jogging. However, you can do most forms of aerobic activities.

Isometric exercises, such as pushing against an immovable force, should be strictly avoided because they raise the BP to unaccepted levels.

Conditioning your upper body can be a good complement to aerobic exercise and may also help lower blood pressure. But the type of upper-body workout you do is crucial. It's generally safe to lift light weights for many reps. Do not use heavy weights as this can raise blood pressure to dangerous levels.

What precautions should you take?

- Do not do any anything that may cause blood pressure to increase: such as smoking or excessive alcohol consumption.
- Check your blood pressure regularly. Before starting, get your blood sugar checked and do an ECG.
- Ensure that you are sleeping and taking medication regularly.
- Join a meditation or yoga class to de-stress yourself.
- Do not use heavy weights.
- Avoid high-impact exercises and all exercises which require severe and unaccustomed exertion.

Diabetes

The best thing a diabetic can do is to stay active. Regular exercise helps in lowering your blood sugar levels. It also reduces your insulin requirement, so control is achieved with less medication. It has the added benefit of keeping your weight under control and your heart fit.

Exercise changes metabolism in positive ways, especially for diabetics who are already suffering from high blood sugar levels. It increases the rate at which you burn glucose for fuel and helps in long-term control and prevention of diabetes-related complications.

What exercises should you do?

Aerobic exercises such as walking, cycling or swimming are best for diabetics.

Weight training can also be done, but remember to follow a high volume, low intensity plan i.e. less weights and more sets and reps.

All stretching exercises are beneficial.

But this general rule needs to be modified in certain cases, according to whether or not, the patient has other complications or features of diabetes.

Decreased sensation in the feet: One of the features of diabetes is diminished sensation, or a feeling of numbness or pins and needles in the upper and lower limbs. These are the cases where a trivial trauma can go unnoticed and complications can set in, or where a small superficial scratch leads to gangrene of the limb, and amputation may be required. Diabetics who have this kind of neuropathy or nerve involvement need to be extra cautious. They should avoid all high-impact sports such as jogging and jumping. Walking, swimming and water exercises would be the best for such persons, provided you are careful. Proper shoes are a must, those that have a cushioned sole and a wide toe box. Wear socks of a material that absorbs sweat. This will keep your feet clean and dry, and prevent infections .

Diabetic retinopathy: Avoid weight training. Sudden rise of intraocular pressure (pressure inside the eyeball) can lead to haemorrhages in the eye.

Poor control of diabetes: Those who have erratic bloodsugar levels should avoid all potentially risky activities such as rock climbing, diving or bungee jumping as an attack of hypoglycemia will be difficult to manage. Adventure sports are not recommended for such cases.

Heart problems related to diabetes: *Refer to the section on exercise with heart diseases.*

What precautions should you take?

- Visit a doctor. Get your blood sugar under control.
- Get your ECG and stress test done to see how well the heart is functioning.
- Check your blood sugar before and after a workout.
- Work out for 20 minutes only, not longer. If you want to prolong the session, check your blood sugar in between.
- Hydrate yourself with plenty of liquids. Drink lots of water. Have about 500 millilitres 2 hours before exercise. During the workout, keep sipping liquids so that you replace what you have lost in sweat. Water is the best, unless you have started with symptoms of hypoglycemia, then it is better to take a sugary drink such as fruit juice or glucose in water.
- If your blood sugar is under 100 mg/dl, have a snack containing 15–30 grams of carbohydrate before you exercise.
- If your blood sugar is excessive (over 250 mg/dl for people with Type 2 diabetes; over 200 mg/dl for those with Type 1), postpone vigorous exercise until you bring it down to an acceptable level. Walk instead.
- Know the signs of hypoglycemia (for example, dizziness, sweating, faintness trembling, double vision), and have a high-calorie snack ready if they occur. It is best to have packets of sugar or sugar cubes handy when you are exercising.
- Inform your trainers, colleagues and exercise partners that you are diabetic. Tell them what needs to be done in an emergency. Avoid exercising by yourself. Wear an identification tag, or carry a card declaring your diabetic status.
- Do not exercise on an empty stomach. Exercise 1–2 hours after a meal. If it has been more than 4 hours since you had your last meal, have a snack before you start.

- Avoid exercise at times of peak insulin activity. Avoid exercise 3 hours after a short-acting and 12 hours after a long-acting insulin dose. For most diabetics, morning exercise is the best. People who have Type 1 diabetes should avoid evening exercise.
- Anaerobic exercises utilize glycogen reserves. You need extra carbohydrates after anaerobic or prolonged exercise, especially if you have been doing sit ups and push ups, heavy cycling or endurance running. A single carbohydrate meal might not be enough. You may need extra carbohydrate foods for up to 24 hours to refill muscle starch reserves. If this requirement is not fulfilled you may suffer from what is known as delayed hypoglycemia.
- Avoid alcohol around the time of exercise (even the night before a morning workout).
- Be aware of your own blood sugar patterns.

Exercise while Travelling

Many times we return from an otherwise joyful holiday feeling flabby, overfed, out of shape, and consequently grumpy. Lack of facilities or simply the focus on having fun may mean that you never work out. It seems that travel was designed to disrupt your daily routine, exercise programme and diet. The result can be stress and fatigue that decrease motivation and dampen your desire to exercise. A regular exercise schedule is especially difficult for those who need to travel frequently on work.

However, this need not be so, if you plan properly:

- **Be practical**: It might not be possible to work out at full intensity away from home or your usual gym, but settle for half measures. It is better to walk 1 kilometre—instead of your usual 5—than not walk at all. It is better to work out once or twice a week, rather than not work out for the whole duration of your trip. Some form of exercise is better than none, so lower your expectations. Reset your goals according to what you think you will be able to achieve.
- **Plan beforehand:** Pack some basic exercise gear: walking shoes, a tracksuit, a swimming costume, a skipping rope and a pair of dumbbells.
- **Make full use of the facilities** you do have: Most hotels have gyms, health clubs and swimming pools, which are far closer at hand that most people have access to at home. You can do aerobic

and simple stepping exercises, and weights in your room while watching TV. If none of this is possible, walk fast around the hotel. Take the stairs instead of the lift or escalator.

- **Take a skipping rope**: Skipping is good exercise, can be done in your room, and requires minimum investment by way of money, time and space.
- **Choose a destination when travelling on vacation** that gives you the chance to work out, rather than loll in your hotel suite, eating and drinking. If you are sightseeing, walk rather than taking a bus or taxi. Go on a walking holiday in some scenic spot, or go trekking in the hills. Rowing, rafting, mountain climbing, diving, water-skiing and beach games are all forms of exercise which most people get to experience only on vacation.

It is not advisable to start an exercise programme while you are travelling. While travelling, you need to be flexible and improvise as you go along. Remember that consistency is the key to success.

A word of caution
If you are walking in the mountains, go uphill first. You should walk downhill on your way back. Be careful of weather conditions. If you are walking at night, check for visibility and safety.
If you are walking on a beach, or doing simple water exercises, walk where the ground feels firm, not where your feet sink into the sand.

A Mini Workout

This is a highly effective exercise plan that gives you maximum benefit in minimum time. It is short in duration but high in intensity.

A word of caution
This workout is for those who are used to regular level of reasonably intense exercise programmes. If you are not of that category, you should not try this. At best you can adapt this to your level of fitness.

- **Aerobic**: Run at a faster speed, for a shorter distance. If, for example, you jog or walk briskly for 5 kilometres, cut it down to a 1-kilometre dash. If you are not used to running, be careful. Choose a soft track as cement is hard on the knees and ankles.
- **Anaerobic**: Use barbells or dumbbells that are lighter than what you usually

use. Do as many reps as you can in 30 seconds, then rest for 30 seconds. If you are hard pressed for time, switch to another exercise without the rest interval. Exercise all muscle groups in this manner.

A word of caution

High intensity workouts can be hard on soft tissues and joints alike, even for those who exercise regularly. A proper warm up is therefore very important.

If you are not an absolute beginner and have reached the level of Week 4 or Week 5 of the beginners' menu, you can try the following workout:

Time	*Category*	*Exercises*	*Notes*
30 seconds 30 seconds	Warm up	Arm swings Side arm reach	Do as many as you can in the allotted time
1 minute (optional)	Stretching		You can skip stretching if you have very little time
2 minutes 2 minutes	Aerobics	Spot jogging or running Skipping	Work out at a fast pace
30 seconds 30 seconds 30 seconds 30 seconds	Strength	Dumbbell curls Shoulder press Flat bench press Triceps curls	Do as many as you can in the allotted time
30 seconds (optional)	Cool down		You can skip cooling down if you have very little time

If you are working out at the advanced level, you can try the following workout:

Time	*Category*	*Exercises*	*Notes*
1 minute	Warm up	Jumping jacks	Do as many as you can in the allotted time
1 minute (optional)	Stretching		You can skip stretching if you have very little time
2 minutes 2 minutes	Aerobics	Spot jogging or running Skipping	Work out at a fast pace

30 seconds 30 seconds 30 seconds 30 seconds	Strength	Lateral raise Forward raise Shoulder press Double crunches	Do as many as you can in the allotted time
30 seconds (optional)	Cool down		You can skip cooling down if you have very little time

You can alternate 30 seconds of strength exercises with 1 minute of aerobic exercise. This will minimize fatigue and be easier on the muscles and joints.

Appendix: The Language of Fitness

Fitness training has a language all its own. Sometimes it may seem that your trainer is speaking in a foreign tongue. To understand what is being said in books and magazines and by your trainer, it is important to know the meaning of various terms and expressions.

Abduction: Moving a limb away from the middle axis of the body; e.g. lifting arms outwards.

Abs: Slang for abdominal muscles.

Acclimatization: The body's gradual adaptation to a changed environment, such as higher temperatures or high altitudes. Certain physiological changes take place in the body due to acclimatization.

Actin: One of the fibrous protein constituents of the protein complex actomyosin. When combined with myosin, it forms actomyosin, the contractile constituent of muscle.

Actomyosin: The protein involved in muscle contraction and relaxation which is composed of actin and myosin protein filaments.

Acute: Sudden, short-term, sharp or severe; e.g. acute attack of pain.

Adaptation: The changes in of the body (or mind) to achieve a greater degree of adjustment to its environment. Adaptations are more long lasting than the immediate response to the new stimuli of the environment.

Adaptogens: These help the body cope with stress through biochemical support of the adrenal glands.

Adduction: Movement of a limb towards the middle axis of the body; e.g., returning arms to the side from extended position at shoulders.

Adenosine triphosphate (ATP): The body's energizer, an organic compound present in body cells and muscle fibres that is broken down through a variety of enzymatic processes. The resultant spark of energy released, stimulates hundreds of microscopic filaments within each cell, triggering muscle contraction.

Adherence/compliance: Used to describe a person's continuation in an exercise programme.

Adipose tissue: Fat tissue.

Aerobic: A sustained activity that relies on oxygen for energy, builds endurance, burns fat and strengthens and conditions the cardiovascular system.

Aerobic endurance: The ability to continue aerobic activity over a period of time.

Agility: Your ability to combine strength and dynamic balance in performing a series of directional changes in rapid succession. Zigzag running is an example of agile movement .

Amino acids: The building blocks of protein. There are twenty-four amino acids, which form a countless number of different proteins. They all contain nitrogen, oxygen, carbon and hydrogen. Essential for protein synthesis.

Anabolic: Pertaining to the putting together of complex substances from simpler ones, especially to the building of body proteins from amino acids.

Anabolic-androgenic steroids (AAS): A group of synthetic, testosterone-like hormones that promote anabolism, including muscle hypertrophy. Medical uses include promotion of tissue repair in severely debilitated patients. Their use in athletics is banned by almost all international sports governing bodies.

Anabolism: The metabolic processes which build up living body substances, that is, the synthesis of complex substances from simple ones. Example: muscle-building by combining amino acids together. Anabolism is the opposite of catabolism.

Anaerobic: High-intensity exercise that burns glycogen for energy, instead of oxygen. Anaerobic exercise creates a temporary oxygen debt by consuming more oxygen than the body can supply. These are short-term (usually highly intense) activities.

Anaerobic strength endurance: The capacity for repetitive muscular capacity such as required in boxing, wrestling and high repetition training (more than 20 reps), and involves the development of severe oxygen debt.

Anaerobic threshold: The point where increasing energy demands of exercise cannot be met by the use of oxygen, and an oxygen debt begins to be incurred.

Anatomy: The science of the structure of the human body.

Angina: A gripping, choking or suffocating pain in the chest (angina pectoris), caused most often by insufficient flow of oxygen to the heart during exercise or excitement. Seek medical aid.

Anthropometry: The science dealing with the measurement (size, weight, proportions) of the human body.

Aquatics: Exercise or sports activities in or on water.

Arrhythmia: Any abnormal rhythm of the heartbeat. Seek medical aid.

Arteriosclerosis: Thickening and hardening of the artery walls, which may cause hypertension or ischemic heart disease.

Artery: Vessel which carries oxygenated blood away from the heart to the tissues of the body.

Arthritis: Inflammation of the joints leading to pain and stiffness, and limited motion. May be localized to one joint, or part of a disease, such as rheumatoid arthritis, which can affect all age groups.

Atrophy: Withering away or decrease in size and functional ability of bodily tissues, muscles or organs—typically resulting from disuse or disease.

Back-cycling: Cutting back on either numbers of sets, reps or amount of weight while doing weight training.

Ballistic movement: An exercise or sports-related movement in which a part of the body is 'thrown' against the resistance of antagonist muscles or a joint.

Ballistic training: Exercises which incur ballistic movements, performed in a graded manner, but in such a way that the athlete learns to minimize trauma to the ligaments and tendons.

Bar: The metal rod that forms the handle of a barbell or dumbbell.

Barbell: A basic piece of equipment used in strength training. It consists of a bar, sleeve, collars and detachable weights or plates. Barbells can be of a fixed weight or a variable weight. The bar is such that both hands are required for lifting, unlike dumbbells which can be lifted with one hand.

Basal metabolic rate (BMR): The rate at which the body burns calories while at complete rest (lying down but not sleeping) over a 24-hour period.

Biomechanics: The study of the mechanical aspects of physical movement, such as torque, drag and posture, which are used to enhance athletic technique.

Blood pressure: A measurement of the force with which blood presses against the wall of a blood vessel. When a blood pressure reading is taken, the systolic over diastolic value is determined. Systolic pressure is primarily caused by the heartbeat or contraction. The diastolic pressure is taken when the heart is filling with blood between beats. Blood pressure values vary appreciably depending on age, sex, and ethnicity. A typical adult reading may be 120 mm Hg (millimetres of mercury) over 80 mm Hg, stated 120 over 80 or 120/80 mm Hg.

Body composition: The proportions of fat, muscle and bone making up the body. Usually expressed as per cent of body fat and per cent of lean body mass.

Body fat: The percentage of fat in the body. In bodybuilding, the lower the percentage, the more muscular the physique appears.

Bodybuilding: The application of training sciences particularly nutrition and weight training to enhance muscle mass and to improve physical appearance.

Bradycardia: Slow heart beat, which may be a sign of a cardiac problem. But athletes usually have a low pulse rate. A well-conditioned person may have a pulse rate of less than sixty beats per minute at rest, which would be considered bradycardic by standard definitions.

Buffed: Slang for good muscle size and definition.

Bulking up: Gaining body weight by adding muscle, body fat or both.

Burn: The sensation in a muscle when it has been worked intensively. It is caused usually by lactic acid, which accumulates in the muscles during anaerobic exercise, or because of microscopic muscle tears.

Bursa: A cushioning sac filled with a lubricating fluid that alleviates friction where there is movement between muscles, between tendon and bone, or between bone and skin. Bursitis is the inflammation of a bursa.

Calisthenics: A system of exercise movements, without equipment, for building muscle tone, flexibility and physical grace.

Calorie: The Calorie used as a unit of metabolism (as in diet and energy expenditure) equals 1,000 small calories, and is often spelled with a capital C to make that distinction. It is the energy required to raise the temperature of 1 kilogram of water by 1° Celsius. Also known as kilocalorie.

Carbohydrate loading: An eating and exercise technique used to build up ultra-high reserves of glycogen in muscle fibres for maximum endurance in long-distance or long athletic events, where glycogen can become depleted to inhibit work capacity.

Cardiac muscle: One of the body's three types of muscle, found only in the heart. The other two are voluntary and involuntary muscles.

Cardiac output: The volume of blood pumped out by the heart in a given unit of time. It equals the stroke volume multiplied by the heart rate. Stroke volume is the amount of blood pumped by the heart per stroke.

Cardiopulmonary resuscitation (CPR): A first-aid method to restore breathing and heart action through mouth-to-mouth breathing and rhythmic chest compressions. CPR instruction is a minimum requirement for most fitness-instruction certifications.

Cartilage: A firm, elastic, flexible white material found at the ends of ribs, between vertebrae, at joint surfaces, and in the nose and ears. Cartilage provides shock absorption between adjacent bones.

Catabolism: The processes in which complex substances are progressively broken down into simpler ones. Both anabolism and catabolism usually involve the release of energy, and together constitute metabolism.

Cellulite: A commercially created name for lumpy fat deposits, which strain against irregular bands of connective tissue. The overlying skin appears dimpled or pitted due to strands of fibrous tissue.

Cholesterol: A steroid alcohol found in animal fats, which causes the narrowing of the arteries in atherosclerosis. Plasma levels of cholesterol are considered normal are 160–200 milligrams per 100 millilitres blood. Higher levels are known to pose risks to the arteries.

Circuit training: A series of exercises, performed one after the other, with little rest in between. Resistance training in this manner increases strength while aerobic efforts make some contribution to cardiovascular endurance as well.

Circuit weight training: A combination of both aerobic and anaerobic exercises or a routine which combines light to moderate-intensity weight training with aerobic training.

Collagen: The most abundant type of protein in the body which forms tough connective tissue.

Collar: The clamp that holds the weight plates in position on a bar. There are inner collars and outer collars.

Compliance: Staying with a prescribed exercise programme.

Concentric contraction: Muscle action in which the muscle is shortening under its own power.

Concussion: An injury from a severe blow or jar. May result in temporary loss of consciousness and memory loss. Severe concussion causes prolonged loss of consciousness and may impair breathing, dilate the pupils and disrupt other regulatory functions of the brain.

Conditioning: Long-term physical training, typically used in reference to sports preparation.

Connective tissue: A fibrous tissue that binds together and supports the structures of the body—skin, bones, ligaments, cartilage and organs. It also provides a protective packing medium around organs and muscles.

Constant resistance: In weight training, when the weight you are lifting always remains the same, regardless of changing leverage throughout a given exercise movement. Example: lifting a dumbbell or a barbell.

Contraction: The shortening of a muscle caused by the full contraction of individual muscle fibres.

Contra-indication: Any condition which indicates that a particular course of action (or exercise) would be inadvisable.

Cool down: A gradual reduction of the intensity of exercise to allow physiological processes to return to normal. Helps avoid blood pooling in the legs and may reduce muscular soreness.

Coronary arteries: The arteries circling the heart that supply blood to the heart muscle.

Coronary heart disease (CHD): Atherosclerosis of the coronary arteries leads to chest pain (angina) or unstable angina, or even infarction or death of a particular area of cardiac muscle.

Crunches: An abdominal exercise which isolates the abdominals while, at the same time, eliminating unwanted action from the iliopsoas muscles (hip flexors).

Cut up: A body that carries very little fat and is highly muscled.

Cutting up: Reducing body fat and water retention to increase muscular definition.

Dead lift: One of three power-lifting events. A maximum (1RM) barbell is lifted off the floor until the lifter is standing erect.

Definition: A muscle that is highly developed, the shape of which is clearly visible. Body definition means loss of fat, and sharp demarcation of muscles, which appear distinct.

Defribrillator: A device used to stop weak, uncoordinated beating (fibrillation) of the heart and allow restoration of a normal heartbeat.

Dehydration: The condition resulting from the excessive loss of body water.

Deltoids: The large triangular muscles of the shoulder which raise the arm away from the body and is a prime mover in all arm elevation movements.

Depletion: Exhaustion following a workout before the body has fully recuperated.

Detraining: The process of losing the benefits of training by returning to a sedentary life.

Diastolic blood pressure: The minimum blood pressure that occurs during the refilling of the heart.

Diet: The food one eats. May or may not be a selection of foods to accomplish a particular health or fitness objective.

Diuretic: Any agent which increases the flow of urine. Used without proper medical supervision for quick weight loss, diuretics can cause dehydration and electrolyte imbalance.

Double split training: Working out twice a day to allow for shorter, more intense workouts.

Dumbbell: A dumbbell is a smaller version of the barbell. The bar is smaller, and is meant for one hand only. Dumbbells are generally of a lighter weight than barbells. Consisting of a rigid handle about 14 centimetres long, with fixed or detachable metal discs at each end.

Duration: The time spent in a single exercise session. Duration, along with frequency and intensity, are factors affecting the effectiveness of exercise.

Dynamic balance: Your ability to maintain control of your body's centre of gravity while moving or in-flight.

Dyspnoea: Difficult or laboured breathing. Occurs normally after strenuous exercise. Can occur at rest or after minimal exercise in patients with heart or lung diseases.

Ectomorph: A thin person with a lean physique and light musculature.

Efficiency: The ratio of energy consumed to the work accomplished. Exercisers utilizing the same amounts of oxygen may differ in their speed or amount of weight moved in a given time because of differing efficiencies.

Electrocardiogram (EKG, ECG): A graph of the electrical activity caused by the stimulation of the heart muscle. The millivolts of electricity are detected by electrodes on the body surface and are recorded by an electrocardiograph.

Endocrine glands: Organs which secrete hormones into the blood or lymph systems to regulate or influence general chemical changes in the body or the activities of other organs. Major endocrine glands are the thyroid, adrenal, pituitary, parathyroid, pancreas, ovaries and testicles.

Endomorph: A heavyset person with a predominantly round and soft physique.

Endorphins: Brain chemicals that ease or suppress pain.

Endurance: The capacity to continue a physical performance over a period of time.

Endurance running: Running up a gradient, or with a back pack carrying weights.

Energy: The capacity to produce work.

Epiphyseal plates: The sites of new bone growth, separated from the main bone by cartilage.

Epiphyses: The ends of long bones, usually wider than the shaft of the bone.

Ergogenic aids: Substances and practices that improve sports performance. These comprise a host of substances or treatments that may improve a person's physiological performance or remove the psychological barriers associated with more intense activity. Can be nutritional, physiological, psychological, mechanical, physical, environmental or pharmacological in nature. Many of the pharmacological aids have been banned by official sports bodies because of the unfair advantage some substances give athletes during competition and because of the deleterious side effects.

Essential hypertension: Hypertension without a discoverable cause.

Exercise: Any rhythmic activity which elevates heart rate above resting levels, and utilizes a single or several muscle groups. Physical exertion of sufficient intensity, duration, and frequency to achieve or maintain fitness, or other health or athletic objectives.

Exercise prescription/menu: A recommendation for a course of exercise to meet desirable individual objectives for fitness. This includes activity types, duration, intensity and frequency of exercise.

Exertion headaches: Pain triggered by a variety of exercise activities ranging from weight lifting to jogging.

Expiration: Breathing air out of the lungs.

Extension: A movement which moves the two ends of a jointed body part away from each other, as in straightening the arm. Opposite of flexion.

Extensor: A muscle that extends a jointed body part.

Failure: The inability to complete a movement. This usually occurs because of because of fatigue.

Fast-twitch fibres: Muscle fibre type that contracts quickly and is used most in intensive, short-duration exercises, such as weight lifting or sprints.

Fat: A white or yellowish tissue which stores reserve energy, provides padding for organs, and smoothes body contours. Fat is also a basic food group. Fat deposits surround and protect organs such as the kidneys, heart and liver. Fats are the primary substance of adipose tissue. A layer of fat beneath the skin, known as subcutaneous fat, insulates the body from environmental temperature changes thereby preserving body heat.

Fat-free weight: Lean body mass.

Fatigue: Physical weariness resulting from exertion or too much exercise.

Fatty acids: One of the building blocks of fat. Used as fuel for muscle contractions. They aid in oxygen transport through blood, help maintain resilience and lubrication of all cells, and combine with protein and cholesterol to form living membranes that hold body cells together. They break up cholesterol deposits on arterial walls, thereby preventing arteriosclerosis. Fatty acids are necessary for the function of the thyroid and adrenal glands.

Fibre (muscle): The long and string-like muscle cells which contract to produce strength. One muscle is composed of thousands of fibres. They range from microscopic size to 1 foot long. There are several hundred to several thousand individual groups (fasciculi) of fibres in each major muscle structure.

Fitness testing: Measuring the indicators of the various aspects of fitness.

Flex: Contracting a muscle (or muscles) isometrically, as in a bodybuilding competition. It can also refer to joint movement.

Flexibility: The range of motion around a joint, or the ability of a bone, joint or muscle to stretch. Flexibility can be improved with regular stretching exercises.

Flexion: A movement in which the two ends of a jointed body part move closer to each other, as in bending the arm. Opposite of extension.

Flush: Cleansing a muscle of metabolic toxins by increasing the blood supply to it through exertion.

Forced repetitions: Assisted additional repetitions of an exercise when muscles can no longer complete movement on their own. Not recommended for beginners.

Freestyle training: Training all body parts in one workout.

Frequency: How often a person repeats a complete exercise session (for example, three times per week). Frequency, along with duration and intensity, affect the effectiveness of exercise.

Glucagon: A hormone secreted by the pancreas, which stimulates the breakdown of glycogen and the release of glucose by the liver thereby causing an increase in blood sugar levels. It works in direct opposition to insulin. Exercise and starvation both increase glucagon levels. Glucagon produces smooth muscle relaxation when administered by intravascular or intravenous injections.

Gluconeogenesis: This is the process by which glucose for emergency energy is synthesized from protein and the glycerol portion of fat molecules when glycogen stores are low. Athletes are often told to avoid undue aerobic exercise to prevent gluconeogenesis as it consumes body proteins and is muscle-wasting.

Glucosamine: A supplement that aids in connective tissue synthesis. All athletes need such a substance, as the repair and growth of connective tissue is never-ending.

Glucose (blood sugar): A simple sugar, the breakdown product of carbohydrates, that becomes the raw material for energy production inside cells.

Glucose polymers: A low glycemic carbohydrate supplement that delivers a steady source of energy for workouts and restoration. They are available as drinks, powders and tablets.

Glucose tolerance: An individual's ability to metabolize glucose.

Gluteals: Abbreviation for gluteus maximus, medius and minimus; the hip extensor muscles.

Glycemic index: A rating system that indicates the different speed with which carbohydrates are processed into glucose by the body. In general, complex carbohydrates are broken down slower, providing a slow infusion of glucose for steady energy. Refined, simple carbohydrates, which are rapidly converted to glucose, have a high glycemic index.

Glycogen: The common storage form of glucose in the liver and muscles that is biochemically processed as part of the energy-producing cycle. It is readily converted into glucose when required.

Glycogenolysis: The cellular breakdown of stored glycogen for energy.

Glycolysis: The metabolic process that creates energy by splitting a molecule of glucose. It is an important part of anaerobic metabolism.

Glycolytic sports: Sports such as wrestling, boxing, 200-metre dash and other long sprint or mid-distance sprints in which the breakdown of the muscle sugar, glycogen, in order to produce more CP and ATP, is involved.

Golgi tendon organs: Nerve sensors, located at the junction of muscles and tendons, that pick up messages of excess stress on the muscle and cause the brain to shut off muscle contraction. The purpose may be to protect against trauma when a contraction is too great.

Good technique: Accurate movement, well-defined posture, proper holding of weights, specific exercise steps, all constitute good technique. When you do weight training, you should grip a weight correctly. Move your arms *exactly* as described. Swinging movements are poor technique. They lead to wasted effort, and increase chances of injury. Good technique can be learnt by starting with light weight.

Graded exercise test (GXT): A treadmill or cycle-ergometer test that delivers heart rate, ECG and other data. Workload is gradually increased until an increase in workload is not followed by an increase in oxygen consumption; this identifies your maximal oxygen uptake. It enables the prescribing of exercise to your actual, rather than estimated, heart rate or aerobic capacity. It requires medical supervision.

Growth hormone (GH): A growth hormone is substance that stimulates growth, gland secreted by the pituitary (somatotropin) which exerts a direct effect on metabolism, and controls the rate of skeletal, connective tissue and visceral growth.

Haemoglobin: This is a crystallizable, conjugated protein consisting of the iron-containing pigment of red blood cells. Haemoglobin carries oxygen from the lungs to the tissues. Deficiency of this is known as anaemia.

Hamstring: The big muscle along the back of the thigh which extends from above the hip to below the knee.

Health risk appraisal: A procedure that gathers information about your health, family and personal history, and other characteristics known to be associated with the incidence of serious disease. This information may be used to change certain behavioural patterns so as to decrease the risk of disease.

Heart attack: An acute episode of any kind of heart disease. Usually refers to ischemic heart disease.

Heart rate: The number of times your heart beats in a minute.

Heart rate reserve: The difference between the resting heart rate and the maximal heart rate.

Heat cramps: Muscle twitching or painful cramping, usually following heavy exercise. The legs, arms and abdominal muscles are the most often affected.

Heat stroke: A life threatening illness when the body's temperature-regulating mechanisms fail. Symptoms include body temperature over 104°F, red, dry and hot skin, chills, nausea, dizziness and confusion.

Heat syncope: Fainting from the heat. When a lot of blood is sent to the skin for cooling, and the person becomes inactive enough to allow blood to pool in the legs, the heart may not receive enough blood to supply the brain. Once the person is in a horizontal position, consciousness is regained.

High blood pressure: See hypertension.

High density lipoprotein (HDL): A type of lipoprotein that provides protection against the buildup of atherosclerotic fat deposits in the arteries. Exercise seems to increase the HDL fraction of total cholesterol.

Homeostasis: The tendency of the body to maintain its internal systems in balance.

Hormones: Chemical substances which originate in the endocrine glands, and are conveyed by the blood to affect functions in other parts of the body.

Horsepower: A workrate measure equal to 746 watts, or about 550 foot-pounds per second.

Human growth hormone (HGH): A hormone secreted by the anterior pituitary gland. Secretion increases as a response to various stressful stimuli such as heat, starvation and intense physical stress (including exercise). It stimulates anabolism and mobilizes stored fat for energy, thus sparing muscle glycogen.

Hyperglycemia: Abnormally high level of glucose in the blood (high blood sugar). It is the clinical hallmark of diabetes mellitus. Usually defined as a blood sugar value exceeding 126 mg/dl fasting or 200 mg/dl 2 hours after consuming 75 grams of glucose orally.

Hypertension: Persistent high blood pressure. 140/90 mm Hg is generally considered a threshold for high blood pressure.

Hyperthermia: Body temperatures exceeding normal.

Hypertrophy (general): An enlargement of a body part, muscle or organ by the increase in size of the cells that make it up.

Hypertrophy (muscle): Increase in both gross muscle size as well as individual muscle cell size resulting from training (especially weight training). Muscles adapt themselves by adding more protein, water and fat to each muscle cell in response to highly specific forms of stress.

Hypoglycemia: Low blood glucose level. Leads to dizziness, weakness, or even fainting episodes.

Hypothermia: Low body temperature. Usually due to exposure to cold temperatures, especially after exhausting ready energy supplies.

Hypoxia: Insufficient oxygen supply to the tissues, even though blood flow is adequate.

Iliac crest: The upper, wide portion of the hipbone.

Inertia: The tendency of an object to remain in its current state (in motion or at rest).

Infarction: Death of a section of tissue from the obstruction of blood flow (ischemia) to the area.

Inflammation: Body's local response to injury. Acute inflammation is characterized by pain, with heat, redness, swelling and loss of function. Uncontrolled swelling may cause further damage to tissues at the injury site.

Informed consent: A procedure for obtaining a person's signed consent to a fitness centre's prescription. It usually includes a description of the objectives and procedures, with associated benefits and risks, stated in plain language, with a consent statement.

Inosine: A naturally-occurring compound found in the body that contributes to strong heart muscle contraction and blood flow in the coronary arteries. As a supplement taken before and during workouts and competitions, it stimulates enzyme activity in both cardiac and skeletal muscle cells for improved regeneration of ATP. Said to improve performance.

Insertion: The attachment of a muscle to the more moveable or distal (farther from the centre of the body) structure.

Insulin: Peptide hormone secreted from the pancreas. It increases the ability of certain organs, such as muscles and the liver, to utilize glucose and amino acids. Inadequate secretion of insulin results in improper metabolism of carbohydrates and fats and brings on diabetes.

Intensity: The amount of force—or energy—you expend during a workout. Intensity, along with duration and frequency, affect the effectiveness of exercise. In gym parlance, intensity refers to the difficulty of a workout or workout schedule. You can increase the intensity of your exercise programme by adding reps, adding weight, decreasing rest between reps or sets, increasing the number of exercises per body part, or the number of training sessions per day. You can increase the intensity of a brisk walk by increasing speed, carrying a back pack or walking up an incline.

Interval training: An exercise session in which the intensity and duration of exercise are consciously alternated between harder and easier work. Often used to improve aerobic capacity and/or anaerobic endurance.

Intramuscular/intracellular friction: The natural friction between and within muscle fibres caused by contraction. This can be very damaging to the fibres, leading to microtrauma.

Ischemia: Inadequate blood flow to a body part, caused by constriction or obstruction of a blood vessel.

Isolation: Confining an exercise to one muscle or one part of a muscle.

Isometric contraction: A muscular contraction in which the muscle retains its length while increasing in tension, but no movement occurs.

Isotonic contraction: A concentric muscular contraction in which the load remains constant but the tension varies with the joint angle.

Jerk: The part of the Olympic lift known as the 'clean and jerk,' where the lifter drives the barbell from his or her shoulders overhead to a locked position.

Joint: This is formed where two bones come together. It can be movable or immovable. Not all joints have the same range of motion. Structures found at a joint include ligaments, tendon, cartilage, bursa along with synovial fluid.

Joint capsules: A sac-like enclosure around a joint that holds synovial fluid to lubricate the joint.

Kinesiology: Study of human musculoskeletal movement, also referred to as biomechanics.

Knee wraps: Elastic strips used to wrap knees for better support when performing squats and dead lifts.

Ligament: Relatively inelastic bands of white, fibrous tissue which connect one bone to another at a joint.

Local muscular endurance (LME): A muscle's ability to perform sustained, sub-maximum force output over an extended period. It is identical to strength endurance, with the exception that LME is muscle-specific, while strength endurance refers to a complex sports activity or movement.

Macrotrauma: An obvious injury to a ligament or muscle, e.g. sprain, strain or tear.

Maximum heart rate: The fastest rate at which your heart can beat during exercise. To find your maximum rate, subtract your age from

220. For best results, exercise in order to attain 60–80 per cent of the maximum heart rate.

Microtrauma: 'Bruising' of muscle fibres leading to pain, and decreased movement, which has no obvious external change in appearance of the muscle.

Muscle mass: Refers to lean body mass, or the sheer amount of muscle tissue in the body. For bodybuilders, muscle mass is critical. But for fitness enthusiasts, strength-to-weight ratio is more important than sheer mass for its own sake.

Oestrogen: The sex hormone that predominates in the female, but also has functions in the male. Besides stimulation of female secondary sexual characteristics, they affect the growth and maturation of long bones and female responses to exercise.

Overload: This is the extra resistance against which a muscle has to work, the amount by which it exceeds the force which it normally handles. Overload is directly responsible for muscle hypertrophy.

Per cent body fat: The percentage of your total body weight that is comprised of fat. While dietary practices and nutritional restriction are obviously important in controlling this, exercise, especially some form of resistance exercise, is also crucial.

Plates: The metal or vinyl-covered discs that add weight to a barbell. A barbell has a central bar, and weights or plates on either end of the bar.

Power lifting: Lifting of very heavy weights.

Progression: To systematically increase the stress a muscle endures during an exercise. Progression is achieved in four ways: by increasing the weight in an exercise or the number of reps in a set or the number of sets, or by decreasing the rest interval between sets.

Pumped: The swelling that temporarily occurs in a muscle immediately after it has been exercised.

Repetition (Rep): A movement performed in its entirety, e.g. lifting a weight and then bringing it back to starting point.

Resistance: The actual weight against which a muscle is working.

Resistance workout: Any workout where muscles work against resistance. Resistance is the force which the muscle has to overcome in order to complete the movement. All weight training exercises are resistance workouts, as are walking, jogging, or running uphill or with a weighted back pack.

Rest interval: A pause between sets which allows the body to recover and prepare for the next set of exercises.

Ripped: A term to describe a body that has clearly visible muscles and very little fat.

Routine: A defined schedule of exercises, either aerobic or weight training. Planning and adhering to a routine is a must.

Set: A number of repetitions, performed without rest, in a weight-training routine.

Sleeve: The hollow tube that slides over the bar of a barbell, which is often scored to provide a better grip and to prevent slippage and injury when working with heavy weights.

Speed endurance: Your ability to maintain absolute maximum speed while sprinting. It requires both starting strength and the ability to display it time after time after time.

Spotter: An assistant in a gym who is keeping an eye on you and stands nearby to assist you when performing an exercise.

Static balance: Your ability to maintain control of your body's centre of gravity over the centre of your base of support.

Sticking point: For those doing bodybuilding, this is a point in time when a muscle will resist hypertrophy, no matter how much you increase your intensity. This is normal, and can be overcome by a short break or a change in routine.

Weight training: Exercise specifically designed to work the muscles and make them larger and stronger, i.e. to cause muscle hypertrophy.

Stress test: This monitors the response of the heart to exercise, and is used to diagnose ischemic heart disease. Individuals are made to walk the treadmill, and an ECG is taken continuously. If there is a narrowing of the blood vessels supplying oxygen to the heart muscles, this is reflected in the ECG.

Stretching: Exercises which increase the ease and degree to which a muscle or joint can act.

Synovial fluid: Viscous material that lubricates the working parts of a joint.

Target heart rate (THR): The rate at which you want to maintain your heartbeat during exercise. Find your target heart rate by multiplying your maximum heart rate by 65–85 per cent. You should exercise at this level for 20 minutes.

Tendon: Extensions of the muscle fibres. They are slightly more elastic than ligaments, but cannot shorten as muscles do. They connect muscle to bone.

The mirror and photo tests: Take many 'before' and 'after' photos, several times a year. These are your best chronicle of progress.

Training to failure: This is continuing a set until your muscles cannot complete another rep of an exercise. If you keep doing reps without a rest in between, and stop at failure, it means you are training to failure.

The 'eyeball' test: Very simply—if you appear obese, you are obese. Physician and fitness institutions are trained to diagnose obesity at a glance.

Weight: The amount of resistance against which a muscle is asked to work. Barbells and dumbbells all use weights of varying degrees.

Weight training: A form of anaerobic exercise in which muscles are repeatedly contracted against a weight which reshapes the body and builds muscle.

Workout: A planned series of exercises.